NIST 800-171 for

Federal Contract Professionals

New Federal-wide
Cybersecurity Contract Requirements

Mark A. Russo

CISSP-ISSAP

Copyright 2018, Syber Risk LLC
Washington, DC ⊕ Tucson

DEDICATION

*This book is dedicated to my dear friend, **Alan Silverstein**, a loyal and faithful friend who recently moved on to a higher and more peaceful place....*

This book is also dedicated to the cyber-security men and women that protect and defend the Information Systems of this great Nation.

Copyright 2018, by Syber Risk LLC

LEGAL STUFF

**SPECIAL NOTE TO OUR READERS: In June 2018, the NIST issued NIST 800-171A, _"Assessing Security Requirements for Controlled Unclassified Information." It increased the challenges and complexity of the current federal, and especially for the Department of Defense (DOD) efforts, to better secure the national cybersecurity environment. It added another 298 sub-controls (SUB CTRL) that may also be described as a Control Correlation Identifier (CCI). They provide a standard identifier and description for each of a singular and actionable statement that comprises a general cybersecurity control. These sub-controls provide added detail and granularity that bridge the gap between high-level policy expressions and low-level implementations. The ability to trace security requirements from their original "high-level" control to its low-level implementation allows organizations to demonstrate compliance. The impacts of this update are currently unknown and will likely be implemented at the direction of the federal agency and contract office whether these additional sub-controls are answered in part or in total as part of a company's self-assessment responses to this change to NIST 800-171._

No matter how any federal agency interprets and executes NIST 800-171A contractually, the information in THIS book remains relevant to these changes. The information remains specific to the control and provides the reader with the latest information to answer the control requirements with needed specificity to meet the goal of a compliant and secure NIST 800-171 Information Technology (IT) environment.

NIST 800-171 for Federal Contract Professionals

Table of Contents

SPECIAL COUPON CODE FOR: "Introduction to NIST SP 800-171" on Udemy for first 500 visitors at a special price of $19.99   Code: "CYBER-MARK" https://www.udemy.com/introduction-to-nist-sp-800-171

For the Federal Contract Professional

If you are reading this book, you are most likely a contract officer, contract specialist, or contract support individual recognizing that National Institute of Standards and Technology (NIST) Special Publication (SP) 800-171, revision 1, **Protecting Unclassified Information in Nonfederal Information Systems and Organizations**, is an area that you have been recently saddled to execute and understand. Furthermore, you need to ensure contract compliance with several new cybersecurity contract rules and regulations. This book is designed to provide the non-cybersecurity contract professional with the basic knowledge and capability to adequately assess the cybersecurity posture of a prime or sub-contractor that has been required to meet, at a minimum, Federal Acquisition Regulation (FAR) clause 52.204-21 and/or its companion Department of Defense (DOD) supplement, the Defense Federal Acquisition Regulation Supplement (DFARS), and its specific clause, 252.204-7012. This book will provide you and your team the ability to evaluate, assess and determine that a company or business is NIST 800-171 compliant.

Current Cybersecurity FAR and DFARS Clauses

- FAR Clause 52.204-2, *Security Requirements*
- FAR Clause 52.204-21, *Basic Safeguarding of Covered Contractor Information Systems*
- Currently applies only to the DOD (with likely future applicability to a wider number of federal executive agencies):
  - DFARS Clause 252.239-7009, (requires if using a Cloud Service Provider (CSP) that its use is disclosed)
  - DFARS Clause 252.239-7010, (requires "adequate security" [see next chapter], cyber-incident reporting, malicious software and media preservation [see Media Protection section under security controls] specific to the care and storage of Government data, i.e., CUI/CDI)
  - DFARS Clause 252.204-7012, *Safeguarding Covered Defense Information and Cyber Incident Reporting*
  - DFARS Clause 252.204-7012(b)(2)(ii)(D), (requires FEDRAMP certification, see next chapter)
  - DFARS Clause 252.204-7008, Compliance with Safeguarding Covered Defense Information Controls
  - DFARS Clause 252.204-7009, Limitations on the Use or Disclosure of Third-Party Contractor Reported Cyber Incident Information
  - DFARS Clause 252.239-7009, Representation of the Use of Cloud Computing

- DFARS Clause 252.239-7010, Cloud Computing Services
- DFARS Clause 252.239-7017, Notice of Supply Chain Risk
- DFARS Clause 252.239-7018, Supply Chain Risk

First, the prospective company will be conducting its own "**self-assessment**" and providing the contract office with the correct documents and artifacts that demonstrate they are "adequately" meeting NIST 800-171. That does not completely mean you can ignore a review of the submitted package. A level of review, as modest as it may be, still needs to be accomplished by the contract office. This book is designed to walk through the security controls in enough detail for a contract professional to determine whether a business, providing goods or services, to the US federal government are in conformance with these new changes.

Furthermore, while it is not expected that the contract office will have the requisite IT expertise in this area, it will be expected to conduct some level of due diligence. This may take the form of third-party federal or contract services that would inspect the submission packets; don't expect this to occur immediately. It will take time for federal laws and mandates to properly resource the contract community with needed expertise. This book was designed to provide initial guidance and direction on how to understand and assess the 110 security controls.

A "compliance checklist" is also included in the back of this book for the 14 security control families and their specific validation. It is recommended that any company or business submission be reviewed and validated by a member of the contract office or authorized expert to ensure adequate due diligence has been completed prior to contract award. *It is recommended that at least 15% of the controls are physically reviewed by the contract office.*

This book provides the details to determine whether a security control is "compliant," "fully compliant," or "not compliant," to ensure contract requirements are met specific to the NIST 800-171 implementation. The objective is the federal government may provide future requisite subject-matter experts and Information Technology (IT) specialists to assist you, but that they may not occur immediately. This book is designed to help you navigate the NIST 800-171 requirements today.

NIST 800-171 Applicability to Future Contract Awards

Expectations

In late 2018, the expectation is that the United States (US) federal government will expand the National Institute of Standards and Technology (NIST) Special Publication (SP) 800-171, revision 1, **Protecting Unclassified Information in Nonfederal Information Systems and Organizations** cybersecurity technical publication will apply to the entirety of the federal government. It will require that any company, business, or agency, supporting the US Government is fully compliant with NIST 800-171 no later than the date of contract award. The Federal Acquisition Regulation (FAR) Committee's Case # 2017-016 had an original suspense date of March 2018; that date has come and went. The latest and expected timeframe for any final decision has moved to an expected timeframe of November 2018. While it is possible that the Federal Acquisition Regulation (FAR) Committee may further delay NIST 800-171 implementation, the value and the purpose of this book is no less critical.

While NIST 800-series Cybersecurity publications tell a business "what" is required, they do not necessarily help in telling "how" to meet the 110 security control requirements. The number of security controls may further increase based upon the actual or perceived threat to the specified federal agency. Companies will need to confirm control requirements with their respective Contract Office.

NIST 800-171 applies to **prime and subcontractors**. There are three core contractual obligations:

1. "Adequately safeguard" Controlled Unclassified Information (CUI), and if working with the Department of Defense (DOD), Covered/Critical Defense Information (CDI).

2. Provide timely cyber-incident reporting to the government when a IT network breach is identified; typically, within 72 hours or sooner.

3. If operating with a Cloud Service Provider (CSP), "adequate" security needs to also must be demonstrated; usually in the form of a business-to-business contract or Service Level Agreement (SLA). This should demonstrate acceptable due diligence to government Contract Officers (CO).

What is "adequate security?" **Adequate security** is defined by "compliance" with the 110 NIST 800-171 security controls, and when the business is issued the solicitation, i.e., contract award, or when authorized by the designated CO. This does not mean all security controls are in effect, but where a deviation is needed, it is sought by the business in coordination with the Contract Office. This will most likely come in the form of a Plan of Action and Milestones (POAM)[1]. A POAM is required as part of the official submission package to the government. It

---

[1] Developing updates are discussing the requirement of a more streamlined POAM. A Plan of Action (POA) will most likely replace the more stringent federal guidance and direction for NIST-based POAMs for businesses and companies under these expected changes to NIST 800-171 and associated contract clauses' modifications.

should identify why the company cannot currently address the control, and when it expects to resolve the control. (See the supplementary guide: *Writing an Effective Plan of Action & Milestones (POAM) on Amazon®.)*

The business is required to provide timely cyber-incident reporting to the government when a breach into its network has occurred. The DOD requirement, for example, is that the business notifies the government within 72 hours upon *recognition* of a security incident. (See the chapter on the Incident Response (IR) control family).

Additionally, the US Government may require the business to notify cybersecurity support and response elements within the federal government. This may include the Department of Homeland Security's (DHS) US Computer Emergency Response Team (US-CERT) (https://www.us-cert.gov/) or other like agency within the government.

Changing federal cybersecurity contract requirements are also taking into consideration the vast moves within the public and private sectors into cloud services. Typically, the security protections would be found in any contracts or Service Level Agreements (SLA) between the business and the CSP. These are normally sufficient evidence for the government. The good news is that there are many CSPs that are already in compliance with the government's Federal Risk and Authorization Management Program (FedRAMP). Being FEDRAMP-compliant prior to final submission of the NIST 800-171 Body of Evidence (BOE) does, for example, help reduce the challenges of using an "external" or uncertified CSP.

Consequences of Non-compliance

There are several major consequences contractors and their subcontractors need to consider if either unable to meet or maintain their compliance. This can include several serious consequences and it is vital the business stays current regarding any changes or directions from the government that may jeopardize their business relationship with the government. These may include:

- Impact Future Contract Selection. This may be as basic as a temporary disbarment from federal contract work. It could also include permanent measures by government to suspend a company for a much longer time. Furthermore, the government could pursue the company for fraud or clear misrepresentation of their security posture to the US Government. This most likely would occur when an **incident** occurs within the businesses' network, and a third-party government assessor determines there was willful disregard for NIST 800-171 and associated FAR/DFARS clauses. *Remember*, the business will always be assessed against the following criteria:

  o   Was there **adequate security** in place during the incident?
  o   Were the protections adequately established based upon a good-faith effort by the company to protect CUI/CDI?

- Assessments Initiated by the Government. At this phase, the Government will have unfettered access to determine culpability of the incident and whether it further brought harm against the government and its agencies. Cooperation is a key obligation and hiding the incident may have worse impacts than not reporting the intrusion.

- POAM will be required. The government will most likely mandate a POAM be developed to address the finding. This should be a good-faith effort to identify interim milestones with a final and planned completion date to ensure this situation will not occur again. (See the supplement: *Writing an Effective Plan of Action & Milestones:* https://www.amazon.com/NIST-800-171-Milestones-Understanding-Responsibilities-ebook/dp/B07C9T3ZCT/ref=sr_1_1?ie=UTF8&qid=1523295943&sr=8-1&keywords=writing+an+effective+poam&dpID=51eT-dSVLRL&preST=_SY445_QL70_&dpSrc=srch).

- Loss of Contract. Worse case, the Contract Officer may determine that the company failed to meet the cybersecurity requirements and can chose to cancel the contract for *cause*.

The Likely Course: FAR Clause 52.204-21

For very basic safeguarding of contractor information systems that process, store, or transmit federal "contract information," expect this clause to be used in the early stages of NIST 800-171 implementation and transition. FAR 52.204-21 only imposes fifteen (15) "basic" cybersecurity controls for contractor information systems upon which "federal contract information" is stored, processed or transmitted.

> *"Information, not intended for public release, that is provided by or generated for the Government under a contract to develop or deliver a product or service to the Government, but not including information provided to the public (such as on public Web sites) or simple transactional information, such as necessary to process payments."*

This clause variation will most likely not require all 110 security controls and in particular:

1) Cybersecurity training requirements
2) Two-factor authentication (2FA)
3) Detailed system control descriptions
4) Cybersecurity incidents or breach notifications

Expect few federal agencies to apply this clause long-term since it opens the federal agency to both public and congressional scrutiny. Expect this to be applied as a short-term solution with future contract modifications once the agency is more confident in its understanding and application of NIST 800-171.

This book is still applicable for FAR 52.204-21 implementation. It can be used to answer the expected 15 security controls as identified in subsequent chapters of this book. The Contact Office will need to coordinate changes from higher headquarter direction and guidance specific to the actual controls needed as part of contract development and update; companies will need to verify the required security controls with the Contract Office to confirm the needed control explanations as described under their respective control family.

What's the minimum proof of a company's cybersecurity posture?

The basis of NIST 800-171 is that contractors provide adequate security on all covered contractor Information Systems (IS). Typically, the minimum requirement to demonstrate control implementation is through **documentation**. Another term that is used throughout this book is an **artifact**. An artifact is any representation to a Contract Office or independent third-party assessor that shows compliance with specific security controls. It is a major part of the proof that a business owner would provide to the federal government.

The common term for the collection of all applications and supporting artifacts is the Body of Evidence (BOE). The major items required for the BOE includes three major items:

1. *Company Policy or* **Procedure.** For this book, these terms are used interchangeably. Essentially any direction provided to internal employees and subcontractors that are enforceable under US labor laws and Human Resource (HR) direction. It is recommended that such a policy or procedure artifact be a singular collection of how the company addresses each of the 110 security controls.

All policy or procedure requirements are best captured in single business policy or procedure guide. This should address the controls aligned with

the security control families

2. **System Security Plan (SSP).** This is a standard cybersecurity document. It describes the company's overall IT infrastructure to include hardware and software lists. Where appropriate, suggestions of additional artifacts that should be included in this document and duplicated into a standard SSP format will be recommended. (See *System Security Plan (SSP) Template and Workbook: A Supplement to "DOD NIST 800-171 Compliance Guidebook"* on Amazon®)

A *free* 36-minute introduction to the SSP is currently available on Udemy.com at https://www.udemy.com/system-security-plan-ssp-for-nist-800-171-compliance/learn/v4/overview.

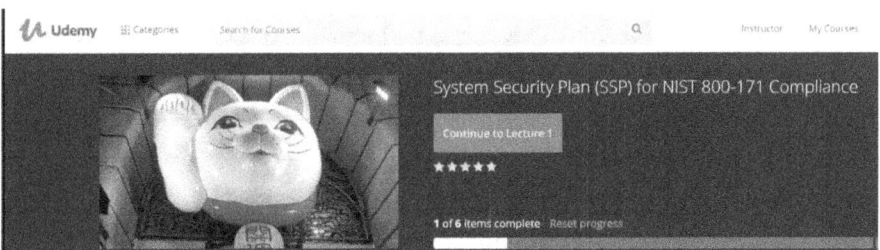

3. **Plans of Action and Milestones (POAM).** This describes any control that the company cannot fix or fully demonstrate its full compliance. It provides an opportunity for a company to delay addressing a difficult to implement technical solution or because cost may be prohibitive.

POAMs should always have an expected completion date and defined interim milestones, if necessary, that describes the actions leading to a full resolution or implementation of the control. *POAMs typically should not be for more than a year, however, a critical hint, a company can request an extension multiple times if unable to fully meet the control.*

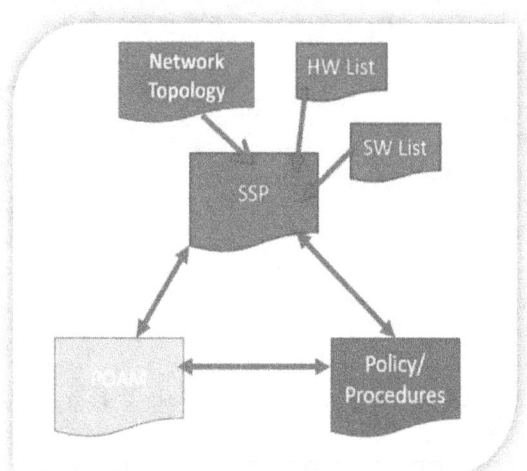

The Major Artifacts Required by the Federal Government under NIST 800-171

Simplicity and consistence helps through
a very young and less-than-defined process

Why pursue an expansion of NIST-based cybersecurity standards?

The Office of Personnel Management Breach

Ongoing intrusions into critical federal systems point to the ever agile and highly impactful effects of cyber-threats worldwide. Reports of the large volumes of personal data exfiltrated from the Office of Personnel Management (OPM), and intrusions into seemingly highly protected networks of the DOD, highlights the need for change. "For nearly a week, some 4,000-key military and civilian personnel working for the Joint Chiefs of Staff [had] lost access to their unclassified email after what is now believed to be an intrusion into the critical Pentagon server that handles that email network…" (Starr, B. 2015, July 31. *The military is still dealing with cyber-attack 'mess'*. Retrieved from CNN.com: http://www.cnn.com/2015/07/31/politics/defense-department-computer-intrusion-email-server/)

The need to implement and enhance the Risk Management Framework (RMF) based on NIST's cybersecurity-focused 800-series, continues to be highly debated. The challenge has been about whether to expand the NIST RMF "framework" beyond the federal government. What if the federal government mandated its applicability to the private sector? This book is written in anticipation of that expansion. Can the expansion of the NIST 800-series, to include specifically NIST 800-171, provide a better means to protect the Nation's sensitive data?

This includes enhancing laws and regulations to increase corporate and business cybersecurity protections; this comprises current laws such as the Federal Information Security Management Act (FISMA) of 2002 and updated by Congress in 2014. These laws, regulations, and processes are intended to improve and protect the critical infrastructures and sensitive data stored within the physical boundaries of the US and its vital corporations. Presumably, such an evolution will better protect the US's vital and sensitive data from both internal and foreign state actors desiring to harm the US.

FISMA was written by Congress to reduce the effectiveness of cyber-attacks against the federal government and its vast IT infrastructure. FISMA and other cybersecurity laws provide a needed method to enhance oversight of information security applications, systems, and networks. FISMA further explicitly sought to "…provide a comprehensive framework for ensuring the effectiveness of information security controls over information resources that support Federal operations and assets" (US Government. (2002). Federal Information Security Management Act of 2002 (44 U.S.C. §§ 3541-3549). Retrieved from NIST: http://csrc.nist.gov/drivers/documents/FISMA-final.pdf)).

DOD Cybersecurity gets Serious

In 2014, DOD adopted the overall NIST RMF 800-series as its cybersecurity standard. In 2017, it officially required its contractor workforce specifically meet the NIST 800-171 requirement. The overall direction has become the current DOD guidance to more effectively protect its own critical IT data and infrastructures, and to expand beyond its DOD boundaries to protect *its* data transmitted into the private contractor sector.

NIST 800-171 will be a challenge for businesses wanting to continue or begin commercial ventures with the government. This book is committed to providing a rational approach that novice through expert IT personnel can effectively answer the 110 security controls. It is through a "good-faith" effort on the part of the company that will protect sensitive data types such as CUI and CDI. This how-to book not only addresses DOD execution of NIST 800-171 but anticipated future federal government enactment of NIST 800-171.

NIST 800-171 revision 1 was the first attempt for DOD that applies to vendors and contractors to ensure CUI/CDI is properly protected from threats. It was further mandated that information about a company's business specific to the DOD is protected from compromise or exploit; that is, modification, loss or destruction. It is attempting to ensure a basic effort is executed to protect the company's own internal CUI as well as co-mingled DOD information that is created as part of the company's normal business operations.

As of December 31, 2017, any company wishing to do business with DOD is required to meet the **110** NIST-based security controls. Companies can implement these security solutions either directly or by using outside, third-party, "managed services" to satisfy the protection requirements of Controlled Unclassified Information (CUI)/Covered Defense Information (CDI). NIST publications while not previously mandatory for "nonfederal entities," NIST 800-171 rev. 1, is the first time that a federal agency has mandated nonfederal agencies, vis a vis, private companies, comply with this federal-specific publication.

"Nonfederal" organizations, such as businesses, and their internal IT systems processing, storing, or transmitting CUI/CDI may be required to comply with NIST 800-171. In the case of DOD, that suggestion is *now* mandatory.

CUI and CDI are not considered national security level information as most typical within the DOD such as **Confidential**, **Secret**, or **Top Secret**. The former DOD terminology for CUI or CDI was predominantly categorized as **For Official Use Only** (FOUO). This data is considered sensitive, but not requiring more stringent security or control mechanisms as with national security information. Basic CUI/CDI may include employee records, Personal Health Information (PHI), or Personally Identifiable Information (PII) protected by federal and state laws. CDI is more specific to the operational and support functions required by DOD to perform its national mission.

The **110** explicit security controls from NIST 800-171 are extracted from NIST's core cyber security document, NIST 800-53, *Security and Privacy Controls for Federal Information Systems and Organizations*, which are considered vital for DOD business and combat systems. Furthermore, this is a highly pared down set of controls to meet the security requirement based on over a thousand potential controls offered from NIST 800-53; this is a more expansive set of controls used by DOD to protect all its systems from its jet fighters to its vast personnel databases.

People-Process-Technology (PPT) Model

This book focuses the federal contract professional on "compliant," "fully compliant," and "non-compliant" recommended answers for each of the controls.   Companies fortunately only need to focus on how to best address these controls to the government—and, it more thoughtfully will help the business protect its sensitive data and Intellectual Property (IP) as well.

The **People, Process, and Technology (PPT) Model** is the recommended guidance for answering many of the controls within NIST 800-171. While all solutions will not necessarily require a **technological** answer, consideration of the **people** (e.g., who? what skill sets? etc.) and **process** (e.g., notifications to senior management, action workflows, etc.) will meet many of the response requirements. **Refer to Control 3.6.1** that provides example responses that could be offered when applying the People-Process-Technology (PPT) model. The best responses will typically include the types and kinds of people assigned to oversee the control, the process or procedures that identify the workflow that will ensure that the control is met, and in some cases, the technology that will answer the control in part or in full.

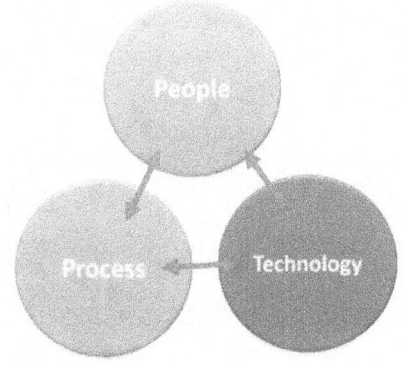

PPT Model

More About Artifacts and POAMs

Other artifacts that are suggested in this book include "screen captures." All current Operating Systems (OS) includes, for example, a "print screen" function where the text or image is captured, placed in temporary computer memory and can be inserted into a documentation application. This can then easily be provided to a CO or security control assessor in the form of either a soft or hard copy artifact. IT personnel should use this function to show, for example, policy settings or system logging (audit) data. When in doubt, always have some form of graphical representation to show the government.

The POAM will be used where the business cannot meet or address the control either for technical reasons, "we don't have a Data at Rest (DAR) encryption application," or cost, "we plan to purchase the DAR solution No Later Than April 1, 2019." POAMs should include milestones; milestones should describe what will be accomplished overtime to prepare for the full implementation of the control in the future. What will the business do in the interim to address the control? This could include, for example, other mitigation responses of using improved physical security controls, such as a 24-7 guard force, the addition of a steel-door to prevent entry to the main computer servers or improved and enforceable policies that have explicit repercussions upon personnel.

POAMs will always have a defined end date. Typically, it is either within 90 days, six months, or a year in length. One year should be the maximum date; however, the business, as part of this fledgling process, can request an extension to the POAM based on the "planned" end date; RMF affords flexibilities. Don't be afraid to exercise and use POAMs as appropriate. (See Access Control (AC) for a sample template).

A Quick Introduction to the Cloud Service Level Agreement

While this book was not written specific to the challenges of how to implement shared cloud services, we wanted to at least present a chapter to the reader for a quick familiarity. While many of us who work in the cybersecurity realm agree that the SLA is a critical artifact in determining third-party responsibility for the implementation of security controls, there is very little information on what a good SLA consists of. This chapter is written for that purpose. If you are writing or reviewing a **Cloud SLA (CSLA)**, or a standard Information Technology (IT) SLA, what are the elements needed to effectively have a good service agreement? What are the kinds of **Service Level Objectives** (SLO) do you need to review as a contract professional?

We will briefly the CSLA's general role, and how to recognize what "good" looks like. Cloud computing is composed of four essential characteristics. They include:

1. **Resource pools** which are available collections of capabilities and functionalities required to maintain a company or agency's services as well as more specifically its cybersecurity posture.

2. **On-demand self-services** that provide the granular elasticity to expand and contract operations in near-real time that is controllable by the customer or System Owner (SO).

3. **Broad network access** which leverages a CSP's larger organic and expansive infrastructure without requiring additional time and resources on the part of the Cloud Service Customer (CSC).

4. **Measured Services** that collect data and metrics to determine the Quality of Service (QOS) provided by and to the customer.

Implementation Offerings & Deployment Models

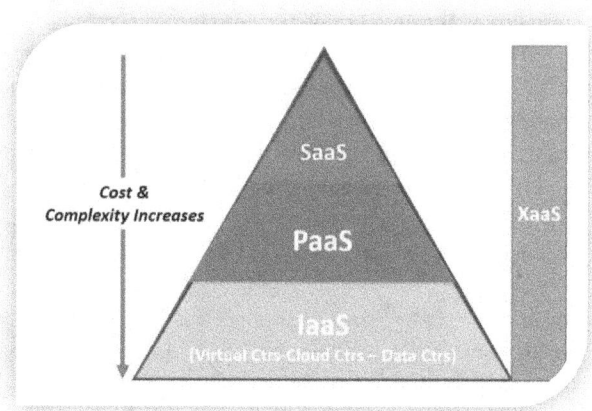

Cloud Implementation Standard Services Model

There are four service models for cloud implementation.

1. **Software as a Service (SaaS):** The capability provided to the cloud service customer is to use the CSP's applications (e.g., word processing, spreadsheet, financial, and human resource) running on a cloud infrastructure. The applications are typically accessible from various client devices through a thin-client interface, such as a web browser (e.g. web-based email). (See Appendix A for a more complete explanation of terminology.)

2. **Platform as a Service (PaaS):** The capability provided to the cloud customer to deploy onto a cloud infrastructure "customer-created" or acquired applications created using modern programming languages, libraries, services, and tools supported by the CSP; these are usually company-tailored applications specific to a unique requirement for that organization and need the proper IT environment that the company or organization cannot develop or maintain organically.

3. **Infrastructure as a Service (IaaS):** The capability provided to the cloud customer to provide processing, storage, networks, and other fundamental computing resources where the cloud service customer can deploy and run arbitrary software, which can include operating systems and applications. This is a much broader model to house

an external and complete IT infrastructure that cannot be maintained or funded by the agency directly. Mostly used to reduce overall IT operations' costs.

4. **Anything as a Service (XaaS):** A collective term of diverse but *re-useable* components, including infrastructure, platforms, data, software, middleware, hardware or other goods, made available as a service. This affords a more "ala carte" approach where services and capabilities can be selected as needed and terminated or reduced based upon operational necessity or cost.

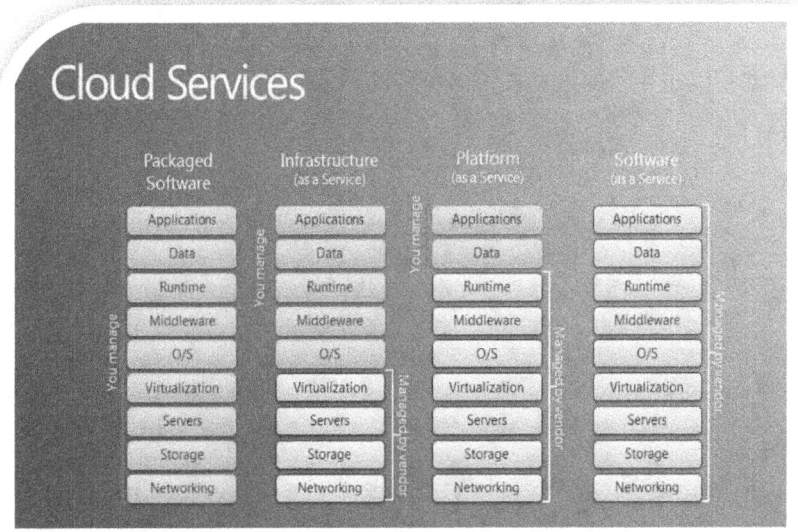

Table 2, Notional Division of Security Inheritance and Risk (Source: DoD Cloud Computing SRG)

There are four cloud deployment models. They are the:

1. Community Cloud
2. Public Cloud
3. Hybrid Cloud
4. Private Cloud

They all have their own advantages and disadvantages in terms of complexity, cost, and flexibility. Considerations of the deployment model should be based primarily on the sensitivity of the *data* (e.g., Controlled Unclassified Information (CUI), Critical Defense Information (CDI), etc.) and the threats against the company or agency based upon current threat information, intelligence and understanding of the overall IT environment.

CSLA Considerations

The CSLA further defines the terms and conditions for access and use of the services offered by the CSP. It specifically establishes the service terms, conditions for termination, and disposition of data (e.g., media protection preservation, maintenance, and destruction policies and procedures) during the period of the contract or upon contract and CSLA termination. The complete terms and conditions for a cloud service agreement are typically captured in multiple documents, but the most significant document is the CSLA. The CSLA, *as part of a well-executed contract*, is the basis of a good cloud security employment. The subsequent guidance and suggested Service Level Objectives (SLO) in Sections 2 and 3 are designed to be the basis of an effective overall cloud implementation.

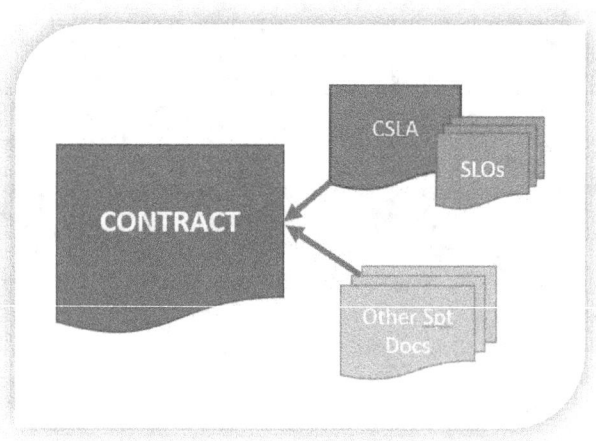

Base Cloud Service Suggested Documents

The CSLA characterizes the understanding between the customer[2] (business or agency) and CSP about the expected level of service to be delivered. If the CSP fails to deliver the service at the level specified, there is a credit or refund that occurs based upon the level and duration of shortfall resulting from the CSP's inability to fully deliver on the stated level or Quality of Service (QOS) provisions. (See Appendix B for a Sample Cloud Service Level Agreement).

Additionally, there are two types of service agreements: 1) "non-negotiable" agreements and "negotiated" agreements. Non-negotiable agreements are in many ways the basis for much of the discussion of the major advantages of cloud, and its economies of scale sought by public cloud computing advocates. The terms of service are prescribed *completely* by the cloud provider. They are typically not written with attention to specific federal privacy and security requirements. Furthermore, with some offerings, the provider can make modifications to the terms of service unilaterally (e.g., by posting an updated version online at their respective website) without providing any direct notification to the cloud consumer.

"Negotiated" service agreements are more traditional outsourcing contracts for IT services. **This should be the objective course for any organization seeking partial or full transition to a cloud service environment.** They can be used to address an organization's specific and "ala carte" concerns about, for example, security and privacy policies, procedures, and technical controls. This could include the vetting of employees, data ownership, breach notifications, isolation of tenant applications, data encryption and overall compliance with international, US federal, state, and local laws specific to cybersecurity protections and execution.

More critical data and applications require an agency to undertake a negotiated service agreement. Since points of negotiation can impact cost and negatively affect the economies of scale that a non-negotiable service agreement brings to public cloud computing, a negotiated service agreement is typically less cost effective. Furthermore, while it may be less cost effective, it can be used to prioritize control protections by the CSP based upon budgeting constraints. It may in fact be a better choice based upon the sensitivity of the data and the company or agencies requirements to ensure overall cybersecurity readiness.

The outcome of a negotiation is dependent on the size of the organization and its ability to exert influence upon the CSP. Regardless of the type of agreement obtaining adequate legal and technical advice is recommended to ensure that the terms of service meet the needs of the organization and the required levels of data security protection required under the law.

---

[2] The term "customer", "cloud customer," and "System Owner (SO)" should be considered equivalent for the purposes of this chapter; they are all ultimately accountable for the security posture of their respective company or agency.

Accountability versus Responsibility

The Executive Order #13800, "Strengthening the Cybersecurity of Federal Networks and Critical Infrastructure" signed in May 2018 held all federal executive branch secretaries **accountable** for agency information security management, governance, and policy; the "buck" was truly placed upon all secretaries and holds them to task to ensure the cybersecurity readiness of their respective agencies.

There are two major participants in a CSLA. They are the Cloud Service Customer (CSC), also called the System Owner (SO), and the Cloud Service Provider (CSP). Typically, the "accountability" for the effective implementation of security controls solely resides with the SO. (See examples of common security controls below.) While the SO is accountable, the CSP is "responsible" for those controls identified specifically within the CSLA; that is why the CSLA is so important to be as complete and thorough as possible. While the CSP will be held to meeting the terms of the CSLA, the SO is always accountable for the completeness and certainty that every control is implemented properly; it is never an excuse to place blame on the CSP when an intrusion or violation occurs. The SO with its organic contract and IT support staffs must understand, draft, and properly oversee its CSLA's terms and conditions with respect to the CSP continuously.

NIST SP 800-53 revision 4

EXAMPLE SECURITY CONTROLS DERIVED FROM NIST 800-53 revision 4, "Security and Privacy Controls for Federal Information Systems and Organizations", February 2012:

CM-9 CONFIGURATION MANAGEMENT PLAN
The organization develops, documents, and implements a configuration management plan for the information system that:
a. Addresses roles, responsibilities, and configuration management processes and procedures;
b. Establishes a process for identifying configuration items throughout the system development life cycle and for managing the configuration of the configuration items;
c. Defines the configuration items for the information system and places the configuration items under configuration management.

IR-5 INCIDENT MONITORING:
The organization tracks and documents information system security incidents.
Supplemental Guidance: Documenting information system security incidents includes, for example, maintaining records about each incident, the status of the incident, and other pertinent information necessary for forensics, evaluating incident details, trends, and handling. Incident information can be obtained from a variety of sources including, for example, incident reports, incident response teams, audit monitoring, network monitoring, physical access monitoring, and user/administrator reports.

Finally, any cloud implementation is no more secure than any standard architecture. It must be managed as any IT infrastructure constantly shifting with changing threats and risks. The sole accountability remains with the SO, i.e., the customer. If there is a failure in protecting its most sensitive data, the fault will lie with this senior corporate official designated. This chapter is written to provide a resource to ensure the protection of vital and sensitive public and private data. Any failure of cybersecurity is not the fault of cybersecurity specialists and IT support staffs, it is a failure of the leadership; accountability must rest with the leadership always. (See the book, "The Cloud Service Agreement: A Supplement for NIST 800-171 Implementation" on Amazon).

All Things Considered

How to use this book?

This book is specifically aligned with the requirements outlined in NIST 800-171's security control families and their specific controls that NIST has deemed vital to secure CUI/CDI. It will help the business to follow the requirements and will assist them to deliver a cogent response to the government.

The focus is to provide the mental approach and technical understanding of what the control is (and what it is not). The first paragraph describes a COMPLIANT control. This is what is needed to prepare a basic answer for a minimal and acceptable level of response. Mainly, these solutions require policy or procedural documents that describe to the government how the business will ensure this control will be met.

If there is a greater desire to understand the process further and demonstrate a more substantial solution, the paragraph, FULLY COMPLIANT is designed to provide more depth. It is intended to more completely describe to the contract professional how to better assess implementation of NIST 800-171.

In the absence of any written company policy or procedural document, or associated POAM, a contract office will have to determine the control as "non-compliant." There is NO PARTIAL CREDIT. A control is either met or there is an associated POAM that addresses how the company "mitigates" the impact of a control that can be potentially exploited by internal or external threats. The contract office may offer extensions for the company to formulate the requisite POAM; this is not as difficult as it may appear. Preferably the company has the expertise in-house to address a complete response, and the contract office can subsequently determine that the control is "compliant."

Also, for clarification, the *Basic Security Requirement* heading is what is typically described as the **Common Control** for the control family. It is best just to understand it is the major control for the respective control family (see the **NIST 800-171 SECURITY REQUIREMENT FAMILIES**). The *Derived Security Requirements* can be considered more as supplemental and "more granular" requirements for the "parent" control. Depending on the types and kinds of data stored, these controls in the more *classic* NIST 800-53 publication can include hundreds of other controls; the US Government has fortunately deemed only 110 controls as necessary.

FAMILY	FAMILY
(AC) Access Control	(MP) Media Protection
(AT) Awareness and Training	(PS) Personnel Security
(AU) Audit and Accountability	(PP) Physical Protection
(CM) Configuration Management	(RA) Risk Assessment
(IA) Identification and Authentication	(SA) Security Assessment
(IR) Incident Response	(SC) System and Communications Protection
(MA) Maintenance	(SI) System and Information Integrity

NIST 800-171 SECURITY REQUIREMENT FAMILIES

Tailoring-out Controls Possibilities

The 2016 version update to NIST 800-171, revision 1, provides a less-than adequate direction on the matter of **control tailoring**. It states in Appendix E that there are three primary criteria for the removal of a security control (or control enhancement) from consideration and inclusion within the NIST 800-171 BOE:

• **The control is uniquely federal (i.e., primarily the responsibility of the federal government):** The government directly provides the control to the company. While possible, expect this not typically to occur.

• **The control is not directly related to protecting the confidentiality of CUI/CDI:** This will also not apply since all these controls were originally chosen to protect the confidentiality of all CUI/CDI. That's why this book exists to explain better how to address these controls which are for the most part all required.

• **The control is expected to be routinely satisfied by Nonfederal Organizations (NFO) without specification:** In other words, the control is expected to be met by the NFO, i.e., the company (you and your IT team.)

Tailoring is allowed and recommended where appropriate. Within the NIST cybersecurity framework, the concept of **tailoring-out** of a control is desirable where technically or operationally it cannot be reasonably applied. This will require technical certainty that the control is Non-Applicable (N/A). Under this opportunity, if the company's IT architecture does not contain within its **security boundary** the technology where such a control would be required to be applied then the control is identified as N/A.

For example, where the business has no Wi-Fi network in its security boundary, it can advise the government that any controls addressing the security of Wi-Fi networks would be an N/A control. The business cannot nor have reason to implement these security controls because it currently doesn't allow Wi-Fi networks or any presence of such equipment such as Wi-Fi routers, antennas, etc. The control would be marked as **compliant** and annotated as N/A at the time of the self-assessment. It would still be required to identify that Wi-fi is not currently authorized in the company's cybersecurity procedure guide or policy to properly document its absence as a suggested best-practice approach for the submitted BOE.

The following Wi-fi security controls most likely can be tailored-out specific to the company's existing IT infrastructure:

3.1.16 Authorize wireless access prior to allowing such connections.

3.1.17 Protect wireless access using authentication and encryption.

Tailoring-out can be your friend

ACCESS CONTROL (AC)
The most technical, complex and vital

Access Control (AC) is probably the most technical and most vital security control family within the cybersecurity process. This too may be the most difficult for the contract office to understand and assess. The assessment by the contract office is best approached as a "documentation review"; that is a totally acceptable approach.

The AC control It is designed to focus computer support personnel, System Administrators (SA), or similar IT staff, on the technical security protections of critical data. The contract office will hopefully have some expertise to assess this complex of security controls. This would include any CUI/CDI and internal sensitive data maintained by the company's IT infrastructure and maintained by the company as part of doing business with the government. If making investments in cybersecurity infrastructure upgrades, the *AC control will provide the greatest Return on Investment*.

Also, it is important to confirm whether either a technical solution is not already embedded in the current IT system. This will more than likely be described in the company's cybersecurity policy or procedural documents.

Many times, controls are ignored, captured by policy, or a POAM is developed, even though some base capabilities to address the control are already resident in the IT system or more particularly within the network Operating System (OS). Also, check for accessory applications provided by the OS manufacturer to determine whether a no-cost solution is already resident. Ask the IT staff to confirm whether there is an existing technical solution as part of the system to avoid spending additional dollars for capabilities already in place.

Where cost is currently prohibitive to implement, a POAM is an acceptable but temporary solution. If unable to address the control during the company's "self-assessment" effort, then be prepared to formulate a Plans of Action and Milestone (POAM). (*Writing an Effective POAM* is a current supplement to this book to be released on Amazon®).

NIST 800-171 Agile Plan of Action & Milestones ©

CONTROLLED UNCLASSIFIED INFORMATION/CRITICAL DEFENSE INFORMATION [DOD ONLY] -- [WHEN FILLED IN]

SYSTEM NAME: [ ]

System Information:

System Name	
Company/Organization	
Sponsoring Service/Agency	

POAM Contact Information:

POC Name/Title	
POC Phone	
POC Email	

POAM History:

Date of this POAM	
Date of Last Update	
Date of Original POAM	

Security Costs (optional):

Security Costs (TOTAL):	
Personnel	
Equipment	

*MOVE Compliant Controls to next tab

*ADD ADDITIONAL COLUMNS for MILESTONE ACTIVITY & COMPLETION DATE AS NEEDED

[1] Status [G, Y, R]	[2] NIST 800-171 Control Family	[3] NIST 800-171 Identifier	[4] Scan Identifier	[5] Weakness/Deficiency Identifier	[6] Weakness or Deficiency	[7] POC	[8] Resources Required	[9] Overall Completion Date	[10A] Milestone Activity-1	[10B] Milestone Completion Date-1	[10C] Milestone Activity-2	[10D] Milestone Completion Date-2	[10E] Milestone Activity-3	[10F] Milestone Completion Date-3	[11] Changes to Milestone	[12] Risk Level (High/Moderate/Low)	[13] Estimated Sec. Costs	[14] Comments
G	AC	3.1.8		System Administrator	No limits on unsuccessful logon attempts	Susan James	None	1-Jun-19	Set policy setting to forced lockout of users failing 3 logon	1-Jun-19						Low	$0	Policy setting update required by authorized privileged user
Y	AT	3.2.3		CDO	No assigned insider security officer	Alice Cooper	Additional budget for one full-time security person	15-Jun-19	Job announcement out on	15-Apr-19	Begin interviews	15-May-19	Select/Begin new insider threat	15-Jun-19		Mod	$180,000	Hiring action approved by President 10 Jun
R			CVE-E234	ACAS	Elbow Bleed Patch missing	John Smith	Patch computer activated	20-Apr-19	Test patch in testbed environment ABC123	20-Apr-19	Deploy Patch to 200 servers globally	15-Apr-19			None	Mod	$0	Testing patch with roll back standard IT procedures
R	IA	3.5.3		System Administrator	Not using multifactor authentication for local and network access	Bob Dole	Equipment, servers, IA consultant, tokens for all employees	20-Oct-19	Conduct research on solutions	5-Jun-19	Recommend to Sr leadership	4-Jul-19	Begin/complete rollout of all equipment	20-Oct-19	Potential if training cannot assist and create classroom instruction, etc.	High	$235,000	May require POAM extension if all PPT components not in place by 20 Oct 2019

Active POAMs | Completed POAMs | (+)

Sample POAM Template

Basic Security Requirements:

3.1.1 Limit information system access to authorized users, processes acting on behalf of authorized users, or devices (including other information systems).
COMPLIANT: Address this control in the business policy/procedural document. (See example procedure below).

It should identify the types of users and what level of access they are authorized. Typically, there are **general users** who have regular daily access to the corporate system data, and **elevated/privileged users**.

Elevated/privileged users are usually limited to, for example, System Administrators (SA), Database Administrators (DBA), and other designated Help Desk IT support staff personnel who manage the back-office care of the system; these users usually have **root access**. Root access provides what is more typically described as **super-user** access. These individuals should be highly and regularly screened. These individuals need to be regularly assessed or audited by senior corporate designated personnel.

FULLY COMPLIANT: This should include screen captures that show a sample of employees and their types and kinds of access rights. This could include their read, write, edit, delete, etc., **rights** typically controlled by an assigned SA.

We have provided an example of a suggested procedure for this control:

> EXAMPLE PROCEDURE: *The company has defined two types of authorized users. There are **general users**, those that require normal daily access to company automated resources, and **privileged users**, employees with elevated privileges required to conduct regular back-office care and maintenance of corporate assets and Information Technology (IT) systems. Access to the company's [example] financial, ordering and human resource systems will be restricted to those general users with a need, based upon their duties, to access these systems. Immediate supervisors will validate their need and advise the IT Help Desk to issue appropriate access credentials [login identification and password] after completing "Cybersecurity Awareness Training." User credentials will not be shared and…."*

3.1.2 Limit information system access to the types of transactions and functions that authorized users are permitted to execute.
COMPLIANT: Address this control in the business policy/procedural document. It should identify the types of transactions and what level is allowed for authorized users. Elevated or privileged users have access to back-office maintenance and care of the network such as account creation, database maintenance, etc.; privileged users can also have general access, but different logins and passwords should segregate their privileges for audit purposes.

FULLY COMPLIANT: This could include a screen capture that shows a sample of employees and their types and kinds of rights. This would include their read, write, edit, delete, etc., rights typically controlled by assigned SA. The SA should be able to provide the hardcopy printouts for inclusion into the final submission packet to the contract office or their designated recipient.

Derived (Supplemental) Security Requirements:

3.1.3 Control the flow of CUI flowing the approved authorizations.

COMPLIANT: Companies typically use **flow control** policies and technologies to manage the movement of CUI/CDI throughout the IT architecture; flow control is based on the types of information.

In terms of procedural updates, discussion of the corporate documents should address several areas of concern: 1) That only authorized personnel within the company with the requisite need-to-know are provided access; 2) appropriate security measures are in place to include encryption while Data is in Transit (DIT); 3) what are the procedures for handling internal employees who violate these company rules?; and, 4) how does the company alert the federal government if there is external access (hackers) to its IT infrastructure and its CUI/CDI?

FULLY COMPLIANT: Addressing this control can further be demonstrated by implementing training (See Awareness and Training (AT) control) as a form of **mitigation**; mitigation are other supporting efforts, not just technical, that can reduce the effects if a threat exploits this control. The company could also include risk from insider threats (See Control 3.2.3 for discussion of "insider threat.") by requiring employees to complete Non-disclosure (NDA) and non-compete agreements (NCA). These added measures *reduce or mitigate the risk to the IT infrastructure*. They should also address employees that depart, resign, or are terminated by the company; the consideration is for disgruntled employees that may depart the company with potentially sensitive CUI/CDI.

Flow control could also be better shown to a federal government assessor in terms of a technical solution. This could be further demonstrated by using encryption for DIT and Data at Rest (DAR). These encryption requirements within NIST 800-171 necessitate differing technical solutions, and Federal Information Processing Standards (FIPS) 140-2 compliance; see Control 3.13.11 for more detail.

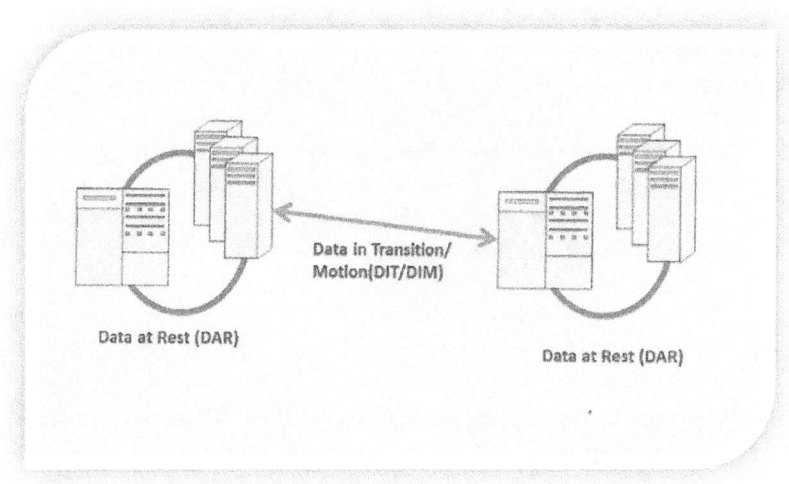

Data at Rest (DAR) versus Data in Transit/Motion (DIT/DIM) Conceptual Diagram

The answer could also include weekly reviews of access logs. Typically, IT support personnel or the SA would conduct recurring audits. If anomalies are detected, what is the procedure to alert senior management to personnel attempting access to CUI/CDI and other sensitive data? This offers a greater demonstration of company security measures to government representatives.

3.1.4 Separate the duties of individuals to reduce the risk of malevolent activity without collusion.

COMPLIANT: This should be described in the corporate cybersecurity procedural document and should identify roles and responsibilities of how oversight will be executed. When this is difficult, based on the size and limited IT personnel, a POAM is highly recommended.

The POAM should suggest other ways used to mitigate such a **risk**, and potentially look at both human and automated means to better address in the future.

FULLY COMPLIANT: Individuals should be assigned *in-writing* and their roles and responsibilities. This could also include the reporting thresholds of unauthorized activities and who is alerted internal threats; this would better provide a more defined solution. It also could address Human Resource (HR) challenges when such incidents occur and provide a means of action against violators of corporate policy.

3.1.5 Employ the principle of least privilege, including for specific security functions and privileged accounts.

COMPLIANT: The principle of least privilege is an important cybersecurity tenet. The concept of least privilege is about allowing only authorized access for users and processes that they have direct responsibility. It is limited to only a necessary level of access to accomplish tasks for specific business functions. This should be described in the corporate cybersecurity policy document. This should also be part of basic user agreements to include what is described in government terminology an **Acceptable Use Policy** (AUP).

FULLY COMPLIANT: Much like the controls described above, a sampling of employees' print-outs or screen captures could show selected and authorized individual rights. A sampling, especially of privileged users, and their assigned roles within the company's IT infrastructure would be a target of potential third-party government assessors. This would be used by assessors to support the developing NIST 800-171 certification process.

3.1.6 Use non-privileged accounts or roles when accessing nonsecurity functions.

COMPLIANT: It is best to always first answer controls from a policy or procedural solution. Essentially, this is preventing "general users" from accessing the corporate infrastructure and creating accounts, deleting databases, or elevating their privileges to gain access to both CUI/CDI and sensitive corporate data. This is about providing the least amount of access and privilege based upon the duties assigned. Companies will see the control below that mandates a separation not just of duties, but access as well based on position and a clear need-to-know.

FULLY COMPLIANT: The more-complete answer could be through automated solutions that monitor access of other security functions such as password resets, account creation, etc. This could include logging and review of all system access. It could also include automated tools that restrict access based upon a user's rights. These technical settings within the tool are established by company policy and monitored by, for example, the local SA.

3.1.7 Prevent non-privileged users from executing privileged functions and audit the execution of such functions.

COMPLIANT: There are many apparent similarities of the controls, and that was originally designed into NIST 800-171 for a reason. Security controls are supposed to be reinforcing, and this control is only slightly different in its scope than others described earlier.

Control 3.1.6 is similar is reinforcing this control as well as others. The company's procedure guide can explicitly "rewrite" the original control description: "Prevent non-privileged users from executing privileged functions...." An example procedure write-up based upon the original control description is provided:

> EXAMPLE PROCEDURE: *Non-privileged users are prohibited from executing any privileged functions or system audits without the authority of the company's Chief Operating Officer, Chief Information Security Officer, or their designated representative. All requests will be submitted in writing with their first-line supervisor validating the need for such access for a limited and specified time.*

Additionally, this procedure limits higher-order (privileged) functions such as creating accounts for others, deleting database files, etc. It also requires the auditing of all privileged functions. It is suggested that the assigned SA at least weekly review and report inconsistencies of non-privileged/general users attempting (and, hopefully failing) to access parts of the internal infrastructure.

FULLY COMPLIANT: A more thorough representation would be to provide copies of audit logs that include who, when, and what were the results of an audit evaluation; these artifacts should demonstrate that the company is following its internal cybersecurity procedures.

NOTE ABOUT "FREQUENCY": Many of the controls do not define how often a business should conduct a review, reassessment, etc. The business owner is afforded the opportunity to "define success" to the government Contract Officer or cybersecurity assessor. The important consideration is that the business determines the frequency of reviews, in general, based upon the perceived or actual sensitivity of the data. This book will typically provide the more stringent government frequency standard, but nothing prevents a company from conducting less often reviews if it can be substantiated.

"Define your own success"

3.1.8 Limit unsuccessful logon attempts.
COMPLIANT: Government standard policy is after three failed logins the system will automatically lock out the individual. Suggest this should be no more than five failed logins especially if employees are not computer savvy. This requires both the technical solution by the corporate IT system and described in the corporate procedure guide.

FULLY COMPLIANT: For example, the additional ability to provide a screen capture that provides an artifact showing what happens when an employee reaches the maximum number of logons would meet this control; this could be added to the submission packet. It is also important to document procedures to include the process to regain network access.

3.1.9 Provide privacy and security notices consistent with applicable CUI rules.

COMPLIANT: Provided below is a current version of a **Warning Banner** designed for company purposes. It should either be physically posted on or near each terminal or on the on-screen logon (preferred); this should also always include consent to monitoring. Recommend consulting with a legal representative for final approval and dissemination to employees.

[Company] Warning Banner

Use of this or any other [Company name] computer system constitutes consent to monitoring at all times.

This is a [Company name] computer system. All [Company name] computer systems and related equipment are intended for the communication, transmission, processing, and storage of official or other authorized information only. All [Company name] computer systems are subject to monitoring at all times to ensure proper functioning of equipment and systems including security devices and systems, to prevent unauthorized use and violations of statutes and security regulations, to deter criminal activity, and for other similar purposes. Any user of a [Company name] computer system should be aware that any information placed in the system is subject to monitoring and is not subject to any expectation of privacy.

If monitoring of this or any other [Company name] computer system reveals possible evidence of the violation of criminal statutes, this evidence and any other related information, including identification information about the user, may be provided to law enforcement officials. If monitoring of this or any other [Company name] computer systems reveals violations of security regulations or unauthorized use, employees who violate security regulations or make unauthorized use of [Company name] computer systems are subject to appropriate disciplinary action.

Use of this or any other [Company name] *computer system constitutes consent to monitoring at all times.*

FULLY COMPLIANT: Another consideration should be this policy also be coordinated with Human Resources (HR). This could further include that all employees sign a copy of this notice, and it is placed in their official file. Select and redacted copies could be used to demonstrate an active adherence to this requirement as a sampling provided to the government. It could also potentially describe how the company can take actions against personnel who fail or violate this warning.

3.1.10. Use session lock with pattern-hiding displays to prevent access/viewing of data after a period of inactivity.

COMPLIANT: While this may appear as solely a technical solution, it too should be identified in the company policy or procedure document. Session lock describes the period of inactivity when a computer terminal will automatically lock out the user. Suggest no more than 10 minutes for a computer lockout. Selecting longer is acceptable based upon many factors such as the type of work done (e.g., finance personnel) or the physical security level of the business (e.g., a restricted area with a limited number of authorized employees) is acceptable. However, be prepared to defend the balance between the company's need to meet government mission requirements and the risks of excessive session lock timeouts.

Secondarily, **Pattern Hiding** is desired to prevent the concept of "shoulder surfing." Other like terms that are synonymous include **masking** and **obfuscation**.

Pattern hiding is designed to prevent an individual from observing an employee typing their password or Personal Identification Number (PIN). This control could include asterisks (*), for example, that mask the true information. This prevents insiders or even visitors from "stealing" another user's login credentials.

Password without Pattern Hiding: PA$$w0rD

Password with Pattern Hiding: ********

Pattern Hiding

FULLY COMPLIANT: The better solution could include much shorter periods for a time-out, and longer password length and complexity; the standard is at least 15 alpha-numeric and special characters.

- Alpha: abcde....
- Numeric: 12345...
- Special Characters: @ # $ % ....

(See Control 3.13.10 for a further discussion of **Multifactor Authentication (MFA)** and **Two Factor Authentication (2FA))**.

As an ongoing reminder, it is critical to place artifacts describing the technical solution demonstrated, for example, using screen capture. It should be clear and easily traceable to this control's implementation by an audit representative or assessor.

3.1.11. Terminate (automatically) a user session after a defined condition.

COMPLIANT: The simplest solution is a setting that the SA or other designated IT personnel, sets within the network's operating and management applications. Typically, most network operating systems can be set to enforce a terminal/complete lockout. This control implementation completely logs out the user and terminates any communications' sessions to include, for example, access to corporate databases, financial systems, or the Internet. It requires employees to re-initiate session connections to the network after this more-complete session logout occurs.

FULLY COMPLIANT: The complete answer could include screen captures of policy settings for session terminations and time-outs. The SA or designated company representative should be able to provide as an artifact.

3.1.12 Monitor and control remote access sessions.

COMPLIANT: This control is about remote access where one computer can control another computer over the Internet. This may include desktop support personnel "remoting into" an employee's computer to update the latest version of Firefox ® or a work-at-home employee inputting financial data into the corporate finance system. Identify these types of access as part of the procedural guide and describe who is authorized, how their access is limited (such as a finance employee can't issue themselves a corporate check), and the repercussions of violating the policy.

FULLY COMPLIANT: The better technological approach could include restrictions to only IT help personnel using remote capabilities. Company policy should require regular review of auditable events and logs. A screen capture would be helpful to show the policy settings specific to the remote desktop application.

3.1.13 Employ cryptographic mechanisms to protect the confidentiality of remote access sessions.

COMPLIANT: *This is a Data in Transit (DIT) issue*. Ensure the procedure requires the company's solution only uses approved cryptographic solutions. The **Advanced Encryption Standard** (AES) is considered the current standard for encryption within the federal government. Also, use the 256 kilobyte (kb) key length versions.

There are many commercial solutions in this area. Major software companies provide solutions that secure DIT and are typically at reasonable prices for small business options such as Symantec ®, McAfee ®, and Microsoft®.

FULLY COMPLIANT: (See Control 3.1.3 for a more detailed representation). It's usually a capability directly afforded by the remote access application tool providers. The more critical issue within the government is whether the application tool company ensures the application is coming from a US-based software developer.

There are many overseas developers, for example, to include Russia, former Warsaw Pact countries, and China, that are of concern to the US government. The apprehension is about commercial products from these nations and their potential threat to US national security. The business should confirm the product is coming from a current ally of the US; these would include the United Kingdom, Australia, etc. *Before purchasing, ensure you have done your homework, and provide proof the remote access software is accepted by the federal government.*

3.1.14 Route remote access via managed access control points.

COMPLIANT: **Managed access control** points are about control of traffic through "trusted" connections. For example, this could be Verizon ® or AT&T® as the company's Internet Service Provider (ISP). It would be highly recommended to include any contracted services or Service Level Agreements (SLA) from these providers. They may include additional threat and spam filtering services that could reduce the "bad guys" from gaining access to corporate data; these are ideal artifacts for proof of satisfactorily meeting this control.

FULLY COMPLIANT: Another addition could also be using what is called a **Virtual Private Network (VPN).** These are also common services the major providers have for additional costs.

Describing and providing such agreements could also identify a **defense in depth** approach; the first level is through the VPN service, and the second would be provided by the remote access software providing an additional layer of defense. Defense in depth can include such protective efforts to prevent unauthorized access to company IT assets:

- Physical protection (e.g., alarms, guards)
- Perimeter (e.g., firewalls, Intrusion Detection System (IDS), "Trusted Internet Connections")
- Application/Executables (e.g., **whitelisting** of authorized software, **blacklisting** blocking specified programs)
- Data (e.g., Data Loss Protection programs, Access controls, auditing)

3.1.15 Authorize remote execution of privileged commands and remote access to security-relevant information.

COMPLIANT: NIST 800-53 is the base document for all controls of NIST 800-171. It describes what businesses should manage and authorize privileged access to **security-relevant** information (e.g., finance information, IP, etc.), and using remote access only for "compelling operational needs."

This would specifically be documented in the restrictions of who and under what circumstances security-relevant information may be accessed by company personnel. The base NIST control requires the business to documents the rationale for this access in the System Security Plan (SSP); the interpretation is that the corporate cybersecurity policy should be an annex or appendix to the **SSP**. (See *System Security Plan (SSP) Template and Workbook: A Supplement to "DOD NIST 800-171 Compliance Guidebook"*on Amazon®)

FULLY COMPLIANT: The ideal artifact suggested are the logs of remote access within and external to the company. This could also be found in the firewall audit logs as well as the remote access software application logs for comparison; these could also be used to identify log modifications that may be an indicator of **insider threat**. (See Control 3.2.3 for further discussion of this topic area).

3.1.16 Authorize wireless access prior to allowing such connections.

COMPLIANT: This would include wireless access agreements and more commonly described earlier is an Acceptable Use Policy (AUP). For example, an AUP would include defining the types and kinds of sites restricted from access by employees. These are typically gambling, pornography sites, etc. AUP's should be reviewed by a lawyer before requiring employees to sign.

FULLY COMPLIANT: The more-complete technical solution could identify unapproved sites and prevent "guest" access. (While guest access is not recommended, it is better to establish a secondary Wi-Fi network to accommodate and restrict visitors and third-party personnel from having direct access to the company network.)

It is also important that the Wi-Fi's network topology and encryption standard be provided as an artifact to the government once the final packet is ready for submission. This should be part of the SSP and the corporate cybersecurity procedure document.

3.1.17 Protect wireless access using authentication and encryption.

COMPLIANT: Ensure this is included in the corporate procedure or policy that only authorized personnel within the firm to have access and that the appropriate level of encryption is in place. Currently, the 802.11 standard is used and Wi-Fi Protected Access 2 (WPA2) encryption should be the minimum standard.

FULLY COMPLIANT: Use of Wi-Fi "sniffing technology" while available may be prohibitively costly to smaller businesses. This technology can identify and audit unauthorized entry into the wireless portion of the network and subsequently provides access to the "physical" company network. Sniffers can be used to notify security personnel either through email or Short Message Service (SMS)-text alerts of such intrusions; if company data is highly sensitive, then this investment may be necessary. Also, maintain any documentation about the "sniffer" and its capabilities; provide it to government representatives as part of the official submission.

3.1.18. Control connection of mobile devices.

COMPLIANT: Most businesses' mobile devices are their cell phones. This would also include laptops and computer "pads" with web-enabled capabilities. This would first require as a matter of policy that employees only use secure connections for their devices when not using the company's service provider—these should be verified as secure. This would also specifically bar employees use of unsecured Wi-fi **hot spots** such as fast food restaurants, coffee shops, etc. Home Wi-fi networks are typically secure but ensure that employees know to select **WPA2** as their standard at-home secure connection protocol.

FULLY COMPLIANT: A better way to demonstrate this control is by discussing with the cell phone provider the ability to prevent corporate phones from using unsecure Wi-Fi networks at any time. The provider should be able to block access if the mobile phone does not "see" or recognize a secure connection. Include any proof from service agreements of such a provision as part of the submitted BOE.

3.1.19. Encrypt CUI on mobile devices.

COMPLIANT: The good news is that all the major carriers provide DAR encryption. Mobile phones typically can secure DAR on the phone behind a passcode, PIN, or even biometric capability such as fingerprint or facial recognition; these are acceptable by government standards. Check service agreements or add to the company's existing plan.

FULLY COMPLIANT: There are several companies that provide proprietary and hardened devices for corporate users. These include state of the art encryption standards and further hardened phone bodies to prevent physical exploits of lost or stolen mobile devices. *Expect these solutions to be very expensive.*

3.1.20 Verify and control/limit connections to and use of external systems.

COMPLIANT: This control requires that all external or third-party connections to the company's network be verified. This would typically take the form of accepting another company (or even federal agencies') Authority to Operate (ATO). This could be as simple as a memorandum, for example, recognizing another company's self-assessment under NIST 800-171. It could also be accepted through a process known as **reciprocity**, of accepting an ATO based upon NIST 800-53—more typical of federal agencies. These are all legitimate means that are designed to ensure before a company allows another company to enter through its firewall (system security boundary) without some level of certainty that security was fully considered. Before an external system or network is allowed unfettered access to the corporations' data, it is critical to identify the rules and restrictions for such access as part of this control.

As always, ensure procedures identify, and limit, such connections to only critical data feeds needed from third-parties to conduct formal business operations.

FULLY COMPLIANT: This could include a request for ongoing scans of the external system and/or network every 30 days; this would be considered quite extreme, but dependent on data sensitivity. If sought, suggest that every six-month that the company receives copies of the anti-virus, anti-malware, and vulnerability patch scanning reports to identify current threats to the external system. This is designed to address inbound threats potentially and to enhance the company's overall security posture

3.1.21 Limit use of organizational portable storage devices on external systems.
COMPLIANT: This is not only about the use of USB thumb drives (see Chapter on Media Protection (MP)), it is also about external drives attached to a workstation or laptop, locally. While thumb drives are more capable of introducing malware and viruses to an unprotected network, external drives pose a real threat to data removal and theft. The company policy should include an approval process to "attach" only company provided drives and highly discourage personal devices attached by employees. Technical support should include the active scanning for viruses and malware every time the portable device is attached to the network.

FULLY COMPLIANT: As discussed in more detail below regarding the use of thumb drives, IT personnel could disable anyone from using the **registry**. Where the need for external drives is necessitated, this control can be further enhanced through auditing of all such attachments and provide pre-formatted reports for company leadership. Auditing, as described under the AU control, should include capturing this activity.

3.1.22 Control CUI posted or processed on publicly accessible systems.
COMPLIANT: This addresses the control of publicly accessible information most commonly on the company's **public-facing** website. There needs to be procedural guidance and direction about who can release (usually public affairs office, etc.) and post information (usually webmaster, etc.) to the website. This should include a review of such data by personnel specifically trained to recognize CUI/CDI data. This may include information or data that

discusses a company's current business relationship with the government, the activities it conducts, and the products and services it provides to both the public and private sector.

This should also address the regular review of publicly accessible data, and the procedure to describe the process to remove unauthorized data if discovered.

FULLY COMPLIANT: This could use automated scans of keywords and phrases that may alert audit personnel during their regular auditing activities. See the Auditing Control (AU) chapter. While this is a static means to alert untrained IT personnel, it could supplement that inadvertent release does not occur. Additional oversight should always be based upon the sensitivity of the information handled to not only include CUI/CDI, but Intellectual Property (IP) or other sensitive data, etc., that may harm the company if released into the public.

The decision process of how much encryption and added protection (such as hashing or emerging blockchain encryption technologies) should be based on the risk to the system.

Consider the risk and the damage to the federal government if the data, CUI or not is compromised

AWARENESS & TRAINING (AT)
A training program is a must

Awareness & Training is about an active cybersecurity training program for employees and a recurring education program that ensures their familiarity and compliance with protecting sensitive and CUI/CDI company data consistently. The contract office will best determine this by a review of a current and active cybersecurity policy specific to the controls within the AT family.

There are several websites (below) that are FREE and government-sponsored sites that a company can easily leverage. A company can use these without expending any of its own resources. The three major training requirements that can be leveraged by most vendors supporting federal government contract activities include:

1. **Cybersecurity Awareness Training.**
   https://securityawareness.usalearning.gov/cybersecurity/index.htm

2. **Insider Threat Training.**
   https://securityawareness.usalearning.gov/itawareness/index.htm
   (More discussion on the "Insider Threat" topic See Control 3.2.3).

3. **Privacy.**
   https://iatraining.disa.mil/eta/piiv2/launchPage.htm (This would specifically apply to any company that handles, processes or maintains Personally Identifiable Information (PII) and Personal Health Information (PHI). The author's expectation is that even though a company does not handle PII or PHI, the federal government to make this a universal training requirement.)

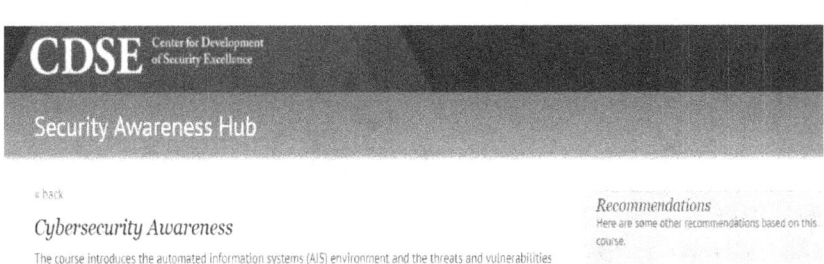

Cybersecurity Awareness

Recommendations
Here are some other recommendations based on this course.

The course introduces the automated information systems (AIS) environment and the threats and vulnerabilities faced when working within the government or defense industrial systems. It provides a working knowledge of cyber intrusion methods and cybersecurity countermeasures to assist employees in preventing cyber attacks and protecting their systems and information. The user experience centers on a single, large-scale, disastrous event. Several contributing scenarios are presented to show different vantage points related to the large event. Through the large event and associated contributing scenarios, students learn about different cyber threats and methods of operation, targeted information, countermeasures, and reporting requirements. This approach demonstrates for users that even small events can contribute and lead to immeasurable consequences.

Cyberprotect

Cybersecurity Shorts

Cybersecurity Toolkit

Security Posters

NOTE 1: A certificate is provided after this course is completed; however, there is no record maintained by CDSE. Students must print or save a local copy of the certificate as proof of course completion.

NOTE 2: Each course provides either a closed caption button (located at the bottom of the course) or a transcript button (located at the top or bottom of the course). This provides a text version of each course section. For any other 508 Compliance/Accessibility inquiries please contact dss.cdseenterprisemgmt@mail.mil.

Defense Security Service (DSS) Cybersecurity Awareness Site

Basic Security Requirements:

3.2.1 Ensure that managers, systems administrators, and users of organizational information systems are made aware of the security risks associated with their activities and of the applicable policies, standards, and procedures related to the security of organizational information systems.

COMPLIANT: Human beings are the weakest link in the cybersecurity "war." The greatest threat is from the employee who unwittingly selects a link that allows an intrusion into the corporate system, or worse, those who maliciously remove, modify, or delete sensitive CUI/CDI.

The answer should be documented regarding initial and annual refresher training requirements for everyone in the company; not average employees but must include senior managers and support subcontractors. Provide a sampling of select employees that have taken training, and ensuring it is current within the past year.

FULLY COMPLIANT: A possible demonstration of the more-complete solution is within the policy specific direction to IT support personnel. There could be a system notification that allows them after notification, manually or by automated means, to suspend access to training is completed. Strong documentation is important specific to awareness training.

3.2.2 Ensure that organizational personnel are adequately trained to carry out their assigned information security-related duties and responsibilities.

COMPLIANT: This is required not only awareness training but also specialized training for privileged users. This is usually Operating System (OS) training specific to the company's architecture. It is possible to have multiple OS's. Privileged users are only required to show, for example, some form of the training certificate, to meet this requirement. All IT personnel who have elevated privileges must have such training before they are authorized to execute their duties.

Additionally, if the company uses Microsoft ® or Linux ® Operating Systems, privileged users will have some level of certification to show a familiarity with these programs. This could include major national certifications for these applications or basic familiarity courses from free training sites, for example, Khan Academy® (https://www.khanacademy.org/) or Udacity® (https://www.udacity.com/).

The government has not defined the level and type of training for this requirement. It requires privileged users to have an understanding and training certificate (with no specified time length) for the major Operating System (OS) the corporate IT infrastructure employs.

FULLY COMPLIANT: If IT personnel have formal certification (such as from a Microsoft ® partner training program), these are ideal artifacts that should be part of the BOE.

Derived Security Requirements:

3.2.3 Provide security awareness training on recognizing and reporting potential indicators of insider threat.

COMPLIANT: The DOD's Defense Security Service (DSS) in Quantico, VA, is the executive agent for insider threat training and support activities. The DSS provides many training opportunities and toolkits on Insider Threat. These are available from their agency website for free at http://www.dss.mil/it/index.html. This is an excellent resource to create an insider threat training program already developed for the company's use.

Document company minimum training requirements for both general and privileged users such as watching select online instruction or computer-based training opportunities from DSS. Everyone in the company should participate and satisfactorily complete the training.

FULLY COMPLIANT: More-complete proof of company compliance with this security control requirement might include guest speakers, or insider threat brown-bag events around lunch time. Company training personnel should capture attendance records to include sign-in rosters. These could be used for annual training requirements specific to insider threat familiarity.

Also, recommend a **train-the-trainer program** where select individuals are trained by either DSS or other competent company that becomes corporate resources. These assigned individuals could provide both training and first-responder support as needed and be deployed to other company sites.

AUDIT AND ACCOUNTABILITY (AU)
System Logs and their Regular Review

The AU control is primarily about the ability of the system owner/company to monitor unauthorized access to the system through system logging functions of the Operating System and other network devices such as firewalls. A System Administrator (SA) is typically assigned the duty to review log files; these may include both authorized and unauthorized access to the network, applications, databases, financial systems, etc.

The contract office will need to best assess that "some" audit logs are produced, reviewed, and acted upon, subject to findings. There should be a designation of someone in senior leadership that reviews such logs on a recurring basis, and for those situations where there is an "incident", that the contract office is notified, typically, within 72 hours. (See the Chapter on Incident Response (IR)).

Most businesses will rely on manual review; however, some "smart" servers and firewalls can provide automated alerts to IT personnel of unauthorized use or intrusion. The key is to understand the auditing capabilities of the corporate system and be prepared to defend its capabilities and limitations if government representatives or third-party assessors request proof of control compliance.

```
usion Detection System

.**] [1:1407:9] SNMP trap udp [**]
[Classification: Attempted Information Leak] [Priority: 2]
03/06-8:14:09.082119 192.168.1.167:1052 -> 172.30.128.27:162
UDP TTL:118 TOS:0x0 ID:29101 IpLen:20 DgmLen:87

Personal Firewall

3/6/2006 8:14:07 AM,"Rule ""Block Windows File Sharing"" blocked (192.168.1.54,
netbios-ssn{139}).","Rule ""Block Windows File Sharing"" blocked (192.168.1.54,
netbios-ssn(139)). Inbound TCP connection. Local address,service is
(KENT(172.30.128.27),netbios-ssn(139)). Remote address,service is
(192.168.1.54,39922). Process name is ""System"".",
3/3/2006 9:04:04 AM,Firewall configuration updated: 398 rules.,Firewall configuration
updated: 398 rules.

Antivirus Software, Log 1

3/4/2006 9:33:50 AM,Definition File Download,KENT,userk,Definition downloader
3/4/2006 9:33:09 AM,AntiVirus Startup,KENT,userk,System
3/3/2006 3:56:46 PM,AntiVirus Shutdown,KENT,userk,System

Antivirus Software, Log 2

240203071234,16,3,7,KENT,userk,,,,,,,16777216,"Virus definitions are
current.",0,,0,,,,,0,,,,,,,,,,SAVPROD,{ xxxxxxxx-xxxx-xxxx-xxxx-xxxxxxxxxxxx },End
User,(IP)-192.168.1.121,,GROUP,0:0:0:0:0:0,9.0.0.338,,,,,,,,,,,,,,

Antispyware Software

DSO Exploit: Data source object exploit (Registry change, nothing done) HKEY_USERS\S-
1-5-19\Software\Microsoft\Windows\CurrentVersion\Internet Settings\Zones\0\1004!=W=?
```

Audit log type examples. The logs above are good examples of the system logs that should be reviewed regularly. These are the business's responsibility to monitor the network actively. Another term of high interest is **Continuous Monitoring (ConMon);** see the article in

Appendix C of the companion book, **NIST 800-171: "Beyond DOD"** (https://www.amazon.com/NIST-800-171-Federal-wide-Cybersecurity-Requirements/dp/198083833X/ref=sr_1_2?ie=UTF8&qid=1526232371&sr=8-2&keywords=beyond+dod) that can be purchased on Amazon. It discusses the importance of ConMon capabilities. ConMon can be accomplished by both manual and automated means, and auditing is a major control family supporting the objectives of this cybersecurity principle.

ConMon activities are best described as the ability of the business to "continuously" monitor the state of its network within its defined security boundary. It should be a capability to determine, for example, who, when, and what are within the company's security boundary and any reporting requirements in the event of an intrusion. It will be based on log discovery of unauthorized activities. (SOURCE: *Guide to Computer Security Log Management*, NIST SP 800-92, September 2006, http://nvlpubs.nist.gov/nistpubs/Legacy/SP/nistspecialpublication800-92.pdf) .

Basic Security Requirements:

3.3.1 Create, protect, and retain information system audit records to the extent needed to enable the monitoring, analysis, investigation, and reporting of unlawful, unauthorized, or inappropriate information system activity.

COMPLIANT: The key part of this control is about audit record retention. The control defines the retention period as a vague capability to retain such records to the greatest "extent possible." The guidance should always be based on the sensitivity of the data. Another consideration should include the ability to provide forensic data to investigators to determine the intrusion over a period.

The historical OPM Breach occurred over several years until OPM even recognized multiple incidents. This included the exfiltration of millions of personnel and security background investigation files. OPM failures while many, including poor audit processes and review, are a major factor in the success of nation-state hackers. OPM's poor audit and retention processes made reconstructing critical events more than difficult for government forensics and associated criminal investigations.

The recommendation to small and medium businesses conducting US government contract activities would be at least one year and preferably two years of audit log retention. Companies should regularly discuss with government contract representatives its specified requirements. They should also visit the National Archives Record Agency (NARA) (www.nara.gov) for CUI/CDI data retention as part of an active audit program.

Businesses should balance operations (and long-term costs) with security (the ability to reconstruct an intrusion, to support law enforcement)

FULLY COMPLIANT: A greater ability to recognize breaches (events and incidents) could include an additional internal process and assigned first-responders who would act upon these occurrences. This response team may have the additional specialized training to include the use of select network analysis support tools to include packet inspection training using tools such as Wireshark ® (https://www.wireshark.org/).

3.3.2 Ensure that the actions of individual information system users can be uniquely traced to those users, so they can be held accountable for their actions.

COMPLIANT: This is about that capture of individual users as they access the system. Access logs should include, for example, user identification information, timestamps of all access, databases or applications accessed, and some failed login attempts. This control is designed for potential forensic reconstruction for either internal policy violations or external threat intrusions. Any policy considerations should include at least weekly review, but any audit review periodicity should be based on the sensitivity and criticality of data to the business's overall mission.

FULLY COMPLIANT: A more complete means to address this control is using automated alerts to key IT and management personnel. This could include capabilities from existing "smart" firewalls, or more advanced solutions may include a **Security Information & Event Management** (SIEM) solution. These are more complicated and expensive solutions, but current developments employing modern Artificial Intelligence and Machine Learning technologies to more proactively identify threats is evolving rapidly; these solutions should be less expensive and easier to deploy within the next decade.

Derived Security Requirements:

3.3.3 Review and update audited events.

COMPLIANT: This is a similar requirement to other AU controls above to regularly review audit logs. We recommend at least weekly reviews.

FULLY COMPLIANT: To more completely address this control, IT personnel could categorize the log types being collected. These could include, for example, Operating System (OS) (network), application, firewall, database logs, etc.

3.3.4 Alert in the event of an audit process failure.
COMPLIANT: This is an active ability developed within the company's audit technology that can alert personnel of an audit failure.

This could include local alarms, flashing lights, SMS, and email alerts to key company personnel. This will require SA and IT personnel to set policy settings to be established as part of the normal checks in support of the overall audit function and control. A description of the technical implementation and immediate actions to be taken by personnel should be identified. This should include activation of the Incident Response (IR) Plan.

FULLY COMPLIANT: Additional technical solutions could include supplementary systems to be monitored. This could include the state of all audit-capable devices and functions. This may also include a separate computer or a backup auditing server for the storage of logs not on the primary system; this would prevent intruders from deleting or changing logs to hide their presence in the network.

These solutions will ultimately add additional complexity and cost. Ensure any solution is supportable both financially and technically by company decision-makers. While to have greater security is an overall desire of the NIST 800-171 implementation, it should be balanced with a practical and measurable value-added approach to adding any new technologies. It should also be a further consideration that the incorporation of new technologies should address the impacts of added complexity and determining the ability of IT support personnel to maintain it.

3.3.5 Correlate audit review, analysis, and reporting processes for investigation and response to indications of inappropriate, suspicious, or unusual activity.
COMPLIANT: This should identify the technical actions taken by authorized audit personnel to pursue when analyzing suspicious activity on the network.

It should also be tied to the IR Plan, and be tested at least annually. (See Control IR for further discussion of **DOD Precedence Identification** and determine actions based on the level of severity).

FULLY COMPLIANT: See Control 3.3.2 for a more detailed discussion of employing a SIEM solution. In addition to manual analysis, the company could leverage the capabilities of newer threat identification technologies such as SIEM and "smart" Intrusion Detection and Prevention devices.

3.3.6 Provide audit reduction and report generation to support on-demand analysis and reporting.

COMPLIANT: Audit reduction provides for "on-demand" audit review, analysis, and reporting requirements.

This should at least use manual methods to collect audits from across multiple audit logging devices to assist with potential forensic needs. Any procedural effort to support audit reduction most likely can use commercial support applications and scripts (small programs typically are explicitly written to the business's unique IT environment) that IT personnel should be able to assist in their identification, development, and procurement.

FULLY COMPLIANT: IT personnel could identify more automated and integrated audit reduction solutions. Likely candidates could be "smart" firewalls or Security Information and Event Management (SIEM) solutions.

3.3.7 Provide an information system capability that compares and synchronizes internal system clocks with an authoritative source to generate timestamps for audit records.

COMPLIANT: The simplest answer is to have IT personnel use the Network Time Protocol (NTP) on **NTP port 123** to provide US Naval Observatory timestamps as the standard for the network; this is considered the authoritative source. The system clocks of all processors (computers, firewalls, etc.) within the company should be set to the same time when first initialized by IT support staffs; this should be an explicit policy requirement.

It is suggested that SA personnel review and compare the external (NTP server time stamp) with internal system clocks. This can be used to identify log changes if synchronization is not the same from the external and internal clock settings. Log changes may be an indicator of unauthorized access and manipulation of log files by hackers.

FULLY COMPLIANT: There are several automated programs that can be used, and good basic programmers within the company could write scripts (small pieces of executable code) to provide these comparisons more easily.

3.3.8 Protect audit information and audit tools from unauthorized access, modification, and deletion.

COMPLIANT: This control requires greater protection of audit files and auditing tools from unauthorized users. These tools can be exploited by intruders to change log files or delete them entirely to hide their entry into the system. Password protect and limit use to only authorized personnel. Document this process accordingly.

FULLY COMPLIANT: This information could be stored in some other server not part of the normal audit log capture area. Additionally, conduct regular backups to prevent intruders from manipulating logs; this will allow a means to compare changes, and identify potential incidents in the network for action by senior management or law enforcement.

3.3.9 Limit management of audit functionality to a subset of privileged users.

COMPLIANT: See Control 3.3.8 for reducing the numbers of personnel with access to audit logs and functions. Maintaining a roster of personnel with appropriate user agreements can afford the ability to limit personnel as well as provide value in any future forensic activities required.

FULLY COMPLIANT: There are several products such as CyberArk ® that could be used to manage and monitor privileged user access to audit information. This product will be a relatively expensive solution for small and some medium-sized businesses.

CONFIGURATION MANAGEMENT (CM)
The True Foundation of Cybersecurity

The real importance of Configuration Management is it is, in fact, the "opposite side of the same coin" called **cybersecurity**. CM is used to track and confirm changes to the system's baseline; this could be changed in hardware, firmware, and software that would alert IT professionals to unauthorized changes to the IT environment. CM is used to confirm and ensure programmatic controls prevent changes that have not been adequately tested or approved.

CM requires establishing baselines for tracking, controlling, and managing a business's internal IT infrastructure specific to NIST 800-171. Companies with an effective CM process need to consider information security implications for the development and operation of information systems. This will include the active management of changes to company hardware, software, and documentation.

Effective CM of information systems requires the integration of the management of secure configurations into the CM process. If good CM exists as a well-defined "change" process, protection of the IT environment is more assured. This should be considered as the second most important security control. It is suggested that both management and IT personnel have adequate knowledge and training to maintain this process since it is so integral to good programmatic and cyber security practice.

Basic Security Requirements:

3.4.1 Establish and maintain baseline configurations and inventories of organizational information systems (including hardware, software, firmware, and documentation) throughout the respective system development life cycles.

COMPLIANT: This control can be best met by hardware, software, and firmware (should be combined with hardware) listings; these are the classic artifacts required for any system. Updating these documents as changes to the IT architecture is both a critical IT and logistics' functions. Ensure these staffs are well-coordinated about system changes. *This should be included in the System Security Plan (SSP).*

Also, NIST 800-171 requires document control of all reports, documents, manuals, etc. The currency of all related documents should be managed in a centralized repository.

Where documents may be sensitive, such as describing existing weaknesses or vulnerabilities of the IT infrastructure, these documents should have a greater level of control. The rationale for greater control of such documents is if these documents were "found" in the public, hackers or

Advanced Persistent Threats (i.e., adversarial nation-states) could use to this information to conduct exploits. Vulnerabilities about company systems should be marked and controlled at least at the CUI/CDI level.

FULLY COMPLIANT: Suggested better approaches to exercising good **version control** activities would be using a shared network drive, or a more advanced solution could use Microsoft ® SharePoint ®. An active version control tool should only allow authorized personnel to make changes to key documents and system changes and their associated **versioning**—major changes within the IT architecture, for example, from version 2.0 to 3.0. This should also maintain audit records of who and when a file is accessed and modified.

3.4.2 Establish and enforce security configuration settings for information technology products employed in organizational information systems.

MINIMUM/FULLY COMPLIANT: There should be an identification of any security configuration settings in business's procedural documents. This would include technical policy settings, for example, number of failed logins, minimum password length, mandatory logoff settings, etc. These settings should be identified by a company's Operating System, software application or program.

Derived Security Requirements:

3.4.3 Track, review, approve/disapprove, and audit changes to information systems.

COMPLIANT: This control addresses a defined corporate change *process*. This should be able to add or remove IT components within the network and provide needed currency regarding the state of the network. This should not be a purely IT staff function. If the firm can afford additional infrastructure personnel, it should assign a configuration manager; this person would administer the CM process.

FULLY COMPLIANT: This could use Commercial Off the Shelf Technologies (COTS) that could be used to establish a more sophisticated CM database. This could also afford a more capable audit ability to prevent unauthorized changes.

3.4.4 Analyze the security impact of changes prior to implementation.

COMPLIANT: Under NIST's risk management process, it requires that any changes to the baseline necessitate some level of technical analysis. This analysis is described as a **Security Impact Analysis (SIA),** and it is looking for any positive or negative changes that are considered **security relevant**.

This analysis should look at any change to the architecture, be it changes in hardware, software, firmware, or architecture. This should be described in the corporate CM process and could be as basic as a write-up from a member of the IT team, for example, that the change will or will not have a security impact, and it may or may not be security relevant.

If the change introduces a "negative" impact, such as eliminating backup capabilities or introducing currently unsupportable software (possibly due to funding constraints**), *it is the responsibility of the company to reinitiate the NIST 800-171 process in-full and advise the government of the rationale for the change.***

See CM control 3.4.4 for a detailed Decision-tree.

FULLY COMPLIANT: A more-complete solution to this control would include, for example, the addition of a new software product that supports vulnerability scans using corporate anti-virus and malware applications or software products. Attach these reports as part of the record.

In the case of hardware updates, the company could demonstrate its SCRM process by attaching proof that the manufacturer is an authorized vendor approved by the government. Access to federal government Approved Products List (APL) may require the Contracting Officer Representative (COR) or Contracting Officer (CO) to approve access to specified databases. The positive review of these databases will demonstrate the proper level of due diligence for any current or future Authorization to Operate (ATO).

3.4.5 Define, document, approve, and enforce physical and logical access restrictions associated with changes to the information system.

COMPLIANT/FULLY COMPLIANT[3]: "Access restrictions" are aligned with the earlier discussed AC controls. As part of a corporate CM policy, any changes to the IT baseline needs to be captured within a formal process approved by that process and documented.

Documentation is typically maintained in a CM database, and more specifically, it would require the update of any hardware or software lists. Proof of compliance would be the production of updated listings that are maintained by the CM database. This should include the updating of any network diagrams describing in a graphic form a description of the corporate network; these are all explicit requirements under NIST 800-171. These artifacts should also be included in the **SSP.**

---

[3] An assessment, while it may appear "easy," is a subjective call by the Contract Office or third-party, independent, assessor. NIST 800-171 only requires a minimum determination of "compliant" as a passing grade.

3.4.6 Employ the principle of least functionality by configuring the information system to provide only essential capabilities.

COMPLIANT: Parts of the government have defined the use, for example, of File Transfer Protocol (FTP), Bluetooth, or peer-to-peer networking as insecure protocols. These protocols are unauthorized within many federal government environments, and companies seeking NIST 800-171 approval are best to follow this direction as well. Any written procedure should attempt to at least annually reassess whether a determination of the security of all functions, ports, protocols, or services are still correct.

FULLY COMPLIANT: The use of automated network packet tools is recommended to conduct such reassessments. Ensure that IT personnel have the right experience and skill to provide a good analysis of this control requirement.

3.4.7 Restrict, disable, and prevent the use of nonessential programs, functions, ports, protocols, and services.

COMPLIANT: Nonessential programs, functions, ports, and protocols are prime attack avenues for would-be hackers. Any programs that are not used for the conduct of business operations should be removed. Where that is not possible, these programs should be blacklisted to run in the company's IT environment. (See 3.4.8. below).

Regarding ports and protocols, this will require IT staff direct involvement in the decision-making process. Certain ports are typically needed for any 21st Century company's daily operation. For example, ports 80, 8080, and 443 are used to send HTTP (web traffic); these ports will typically be required to be active.

Port Number	Application Supported
20	File Transport Protocol (FTP) Data
23	Telnet
25	Simple Mail Transfer Protocol (SMTP)
80, 8080, 443	Hypertext Transport Protocol (HTTP) → WWW
110	Post Office Protocol version 3 (POP3)

Common Ports and Their Associated Protocols

For those ports and protocols that are not required, they should be closed by designated IT personnel. This prevents hackers from exploiting open entries into the corporate infrastructure. Ensure a copy of all open and closed ports is readily available to government representatives for review as part of the NIST 800-171 requirements.

FULLY COMPLIANT: The business could employ tools that check for unused and open ports. This could include a regular reassessment of whether ports need to remain active. As mentioned earlier, products such as Wireshark ® could be used as a low-cost solution to conduct any reassessment of the corporate infrastructure.

3.4.8 Apply deny-by-exception (blacklist) policy to prevent the use of unauthorized software or deny all, permit-by-exception (whitelisting) policy to allow the execution of authorized software.

COMPLIANT/FULLY COMPLIANT: The company should employ **blacklisting** or **whitelisting,** (See Control 3.14.2 for more information), to prohibit the execution of unauthorized software programs or applications within the information system. A copy of the current listing should be part of the formal Body of Evidence (BOE).

3.4.9 Control and monitor user-installed software.

COMPLIANT: The policy should always be that only authorized administrators, such as designated SA's and senior help desk personnel, be allowed to add or delete software from user computers.

There should also be a defined process to request specialized software be added for unique users. These may include finance personnel, architects, statisticians, etc. that require specialized stand-alone software that may or may not connect to the Internet.

FULLY COMPLIANT: This could include as part of the company's normal audit process the review of whether personnel are adding software and bypassing security measures (such as getting passwords from IT authorized individuals). This may also be addressed in the AUP and supported by appropriate HR activities that can be pursued against individuals of any such violations.

IDENTIFICATION AND AUTHENTICATION (IA)
Why two-factor authentication is so important?

The 2015 Office of Personnel Management (OPM) breach could have been prevented if this control family was properly implemented and enforced. The one "positive" effect that the OPM breach caused for federal agencies was the requirement from Congress that these requirements became mandatory. Congress's focus on the use of Two-Factor Authentication (2FA) and Multi-Factor Authentication (MFA) has provided constructive results for the federal government and impetus for more stringent cybersecurity measures beyond the government's IT boundaries.

While some businesses will be afforded, for example, Common Access Cards (CAC) or Personal Identity Verification (PIV) cards to accomplish 2FA between the company and the government, most won't be authorized such access. Implementation will require various levels of investment, and the use of 2FA devices, or also called "tokens." This too will require additional financial costs and technical integration challenges for the average business.

For many small businesses, this will also require some sizeable investments on the part of the company and a clear commitment to working with the government. Solutions could include, for example, RSA® tokens—these are small devices that constantly rotate a security variable (a key) that a user enters in addition to a password or Personal Identification Number (PIN). This solution affords one potential solution to businesses to meet the 2FA requirement.

According to The House Committee on Oversight and Government Reform report on September 7th, 2016, OPM's leadership failed to "implement basic cyber hygiene, such as maintaining current authorities to operate and employing strong multi-factor authentication, despite years of warning from the Inspector General… tools were available that could have prevented the breaches…" (SOURCE: https://oversight.house.gov/wp-content/uploads/2016/09/The-OPM-Data-Breach-How-the-Government-Jeopardized-Our-National-Security-for-More-than-a-Generation.pdf)

The best approaches will require good market surveys of the available resources and be mindful that two-factor does not need to be a card or token solution. Other options would include biometrics (fingerprints, facial recognition, etc.) or Short Message Service (SMS) 2FA solution as used by Amazon® to verify its customers. They use a Two-Step verification process that provides a "verification code sent to the customer's personal cell phone or home phone to verify their identity.

Be prepared to do serious "homework" on these controls, and research all potential solutions. Once this control is resolved, the company will be in a better position not just with the government but have serious answers that will ensure the protection of its sensitive data.

Basic Security Requirements:

3.5.1 Identify information system users, processes acting on behalf of users, or devices.

COMPLIANT/FULLY COMPLIANT: This control should identify/reference current business procedures as outlined in the **AU** control above. It should address that audit is used to identify system users, the processes (applications) and the devices (computers) accessed.

3.5.2 Authenticate (or verify) the identities of those users, processes, or devices, as a prerequisite to allowing access to organizational information systems.

COMPLIANT: While basic logon and password information could be used, Control 3.5.3 below, requires Multifactor or Two-factor Authentication (2FA). The government requires 2FA, and NIST 800-171 requires it as well.

**Remember, if the company is not immediately prepared to execute a 2FA solution, *a POAM is required*.

FULLY COMPLIANT: The better answer is the employment of some form of 2FA. It could be a **hard token** solution such as a CAC or PIV card. The other option would include such virtual solutions that would use email or SMS messaging like Google ® or Amazon ® to provide 2FA; this **soft token** solution is typically easier and less expensive to deploy.   It can be more easily deployed to meet NIST 800-171 requirement.

Derived Security Requirements:

3.5.3 Use multifactor authentication for local and network access to privileged accounts and for network access to non-privileged accounts.

COMPLIANT: See Control 3.5.2 above. Ensure the requirement for MFA or 2FA are part of the company's cybersecurity policy/procedure.

FULLY COMPLIANT: (See Control 3.5.2 for suggested approaches).

3.5.4 Employ replay-resistant authentication mechanisms for network access to privileged and nonprivileged accounts.

COMPLIANT: This control requires replay-resistant technologies to prevent replay attacks. **Replay attacks** are also known as a **playback attack**. This is an attack where the hacker captures legitimate traffic from an authorized user, and presumably a positively identified network user, and uses it to gain unauthorized access to a network. This is also considered a form of a **Man-in-the-Middle** type attack.

The easiest solution to resolving this control is to have company IT personnel disable **Secure Socket Layer (SSL)**—which the government no longer authorizes. Businesses should use the **Transport Layer Security (TLS) 2.0** or higher; it as a required government standard.

If the business needs to continue the use of SSL to maintain connectivity with, for example, external or third-party data providers, a POAM is required. Efforts should be made to discuss with these data providers when they will no longer be using SSL. This discussion should begin as soon as possible to advise the government through a POAM that demonstrates the company is conducting its proper due diligence to protect its CUI/CDI.

FULLY COMPLIANT: A potentially expensive solution could include the addition of a **SIEM** solution. There are many major IT network providers that have added artificial intelligence capabilities to detect this type of attack better; identify any solution carefully.

3.5.5 Prevent reuse of identifiers for a defined period.

COMPLIANT: This IA control directs that "individual, group, role, or device identifiers" from being reused. This should be included as part of any written procedure and defined in system policies to prevent identifiers from being reused. This could include email address names (individual), administrator accounts (group), or device identifiers such as "finan_db" designating a high-value target such as a "financial database" (device).

The reason for this control is to prevent intruders who have gained information about such identifiers having less of a capability to use this information for an exploit of the business. This will help better thwart hacker's intelligence collection and analysis of a company's internal network. This control is designed to prevent intruders' abilities to gain access to corporate systems and their resident CUI/CDI repositories.

FULLY COMPLIANT: Reuse of individual identifiers should be discouraged, for example, in the case of a returning employee. This is a basic suggestion: 'John.Smith@cui-company.com' could be varied examples, 'John.H.Smith2@cui-company.com.

3.5.6 Disable identifiers after a defined period of inactivity.

COMPLIANT/FULLY COMPLIANT: This requires that after a defined time-out setting, the system terminates its connection. The recommendation is 30 minutes maximum, but as mentioned earlier, the time-out should always be based on the data sensitivity.

3.5.7 Enforce a minimum password complexity and change of characters when new passwords are created.

COMPLIANT: If using passwords for authentication purposes, the expectation is that a POAM has been developed until such time a 2FA or MFA solution is in place. The standard complexity is supposed to be at least 15 characters that include at least 2 or more alpha, numeric, and special characters to reduce the likelihood of compromise.

FULLY COMPLIANT: Increased length and variability can be enforced by automated policy settings of the network. Another suggestion is to use passphrases. These can be harder to "crack" by normal hacking tools and are typically easier for users to memorize.

The best solutions are still either 2FA or MFA

The factors:

- 1-FACTOR: Something you know (e.g., password/PIN)
- 2-FACTOR: Something you have (e.g., cryptographic identification device, token)
- MULTI-FACTOR: Something you are (e.g., biometric: fingerprint, iris, etc.)

3.5.8 Prohibit password reuse for a specified number of generations.

COMPLIANT: This is usually set by policy and the designated SA's that limit the number of times a password can be reused; *passwords within most parts of the government are required to be changed every 90 days.* This function should be automated by authorized IT personnel. Suggested reuse of a prior password should be at least 10 or greater

FULLY COMPLIANT: Technical settings can be established for *no* reuse. This ensures that hackers who may have exploited one of the user's other business or even (and more especially) personal accounts, can less likely be effective against corporate computer networks and assets.

3.5.9 Allow temporary password use for system logons with an immediate change to a permanent password.

COMPLIANT/FULLY COMPLIANT: This setting is typically built into normal network operating systems. This requirement for users should be appropriately included in the recommended procedure guide.

3.5.10 Store and transmit only encrypted representation of passwords.

COMPLIANT: This is both a DIT and DAR issue, See Control 3.1.3 for a conceptual diagram. IT personnel should be regularly verifying that password data stores are always encrypted.

This control requires that all passwords are encrypted and approved by NIST's sanctioned process under FIPS 140-2. See Control 3.13.11 for the NIST website to confirm whether a cryptographic solution is approved.

FULLY COMPLIANT: Suggested greater protections could require encrypted passwords are not collocated on the same main application or database server that stores major portions of the business's data repository. A separate server (physical or virtual) could prevent hacker exploits from accessing company data stores.

3.5.11. Obscure feedback of authentication information.

COMPLIANT/FULLY COMPLIANT: This is like **pattern hiding** as described in Control 3.1.10. The system should prevent unauthorized individuals from compromising system-level authentication by inadvertently observing in-person ("shoulder surfing") or virtually (by viewing password entries by privileged users) remotely. It relies upon obscuring the "feedback of authentication information", for example, displaying asterisks (*) or hash symbols (#) when a user types their password. This setting should be enforced automatically and prevent general users from changing this setting.

INCIDENT RESPONSE (IR)
What do you do when you're attacked?

Incident Response (IR) primarily requires a plan, an identification of who or what agency is notified when a breach has occurred and testing of the plan over time. This control requires the development of an Incident Response Plan (IRP). There are many templates available online, and if there is an existing relationship with a federal agency, companies should be able to obtain agency-specific templates.

EVENT → INCIDENT
(less defined/initial occurrence) → (defined/confirmed/high impact)

Incident Response Spectrum

The first effort should be identifying with government representatives what constitutes a reportable event that formally becomes an incident. This could include a confirmed breach that has occurred to the IT infrastructure. Incidents could include anything from a Denial of Service (DOS) attack—an overloading of outwardly facing web or mail servers--, or exfiltration of data—where CUI/CDI and corporate data has been copied or moved to outside of the company's firewall/perimeter. Incidents could also include the destruction of data that the company's IT staff, for example, identifies through ongoing audit activities.

Secondarily, who do you notify? Do you alert your assigned Contract Officer Representative (COR), the Contract Office, DOD's US Cybercommand at Fort Meade, MD, or possibly the Department of Homeland Security's (DHS) Computer Emergency Response Team (CERT) (https://www.us-cert.gov/forms/report)? Company representatives will have to ask their assigned COR where to file standard government "incident" reports. They should be able to provide templates and forms specific to the agency.

Finally, this security control will require testing at least *annually*, but more often is recommended. Until comfortable with the IR "reporting chain," *practice, practice, practice*.

DOD Cyber Incident Life Cycle. This diagram from the DOD will be helpful in assisting a company's approach to IR activities, and will better assist in coordination with government cybersecurity incident response organizations. Recognizing this as either an "event" (not necessarily a negative occurrence) versus an "incident" is an internal determination by the company's leadership in coordination with its security and IT professional staffs. An incident specifically requires alerting the government as soon as the intrusion is *recognized*.

Verify with the respective agency its reporting standards. Typically, **events** may not need to be reported based on the expansive impacts and workloads to government cybersecurity response organizations. In the case of **incidents**, the standard is 72-hours; however, the recommendation is *as soon as possible* due to the potential impacts beyond the company's own IT infrastructure. It can pose a serious direct threat to federal agency IT environments. Always verify this with the assigned Contract Office represenative.

The chart below categorizes current DOD precedence.

Precedence	Category	Description
0	0	Training and Exercises
1	1	Root Level Intrusion (Incident)
2	2	User Level Intrusion (Incident)
3	4	Denial of Service (Incident)
4	7	Malicious Logic (Incident)
5	3	Unsuccessful Activity Attempt (Event)
6	5	Non-Compliance Activity (Event)
7	6	Reconnaissance (Event)
8	8	Investigating (Event)
9	9	Explained Anomaly (Event)

DOD Precedence Categorization. Nine (9) is the lowest event where little is known, and IT personnel are attempting to determine whether this activity should be elevated to alert company leadership or to "close it out." One (1) is a deep attack. It identifies that the incident has gained "root" access. This level of incident is critical since an intruder has nearly unlimited access to the network and its data. (SOURCE: Cyber Incident Handling Program, CJCSM 6510.01B, 18 December 2014, http://www.jcs.mil/Portals/36/Documents/Library/Manuals/m651001.pdf?ver=2016-02-05-175710-897)

Basic Security Requirements:

3.6.1 Establish an operational incident-handling capability for organizational information systems that includes adequate preparation, detection, analysis, containment, recovery, and user response activities.
COMPLIANT: This control addresses a "capability" that needs to be established to respond to events and incidents within the firm's IT security boundary.

This should include the **People, Process, and Technology (PPT) Model** as a recommended guide for answering many of the controls within NIST 800-171. While solutions will not necessarily require a technological answer, consideration of the people (e.g., who? what skill sets? etc.) and process (e.g., notifications to senior management, action workflows, etc.) will meet many of the response requirements.

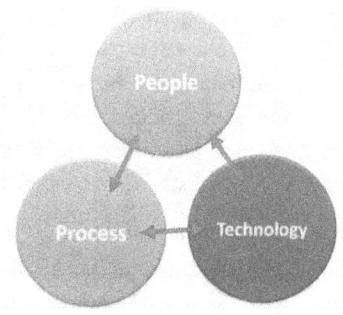

PPT Model

Use the Cyber Incident **Life Cycle** above to guide the company's operational incident-handling artifact/procedure. This should be an annex to the **SSP**. (See System Security Plan (SSP) Template and Workbook: A Supplement to "DOD NIST 800-171 Compliance Guidebook"on Amazon®). The **PPT Model** can be used to guide and formulate the IRP annex. A suggested approach using the PPT Model is described below, and includes the kinds of questions that should be answered to demonstrate best how best to formulate a good IRP:

- Preparation
  - People: Who will perform the action or activity? Training needed? Skill sets?
  - Process: Training policies for cybersecurity and IT professionals to support the IRP
  - Technology: What technology already exists to support IR? What technologies are needed?

- Detection
    - People: Are IT staff able to use audit tools properly to detect intrusions?
    - Process: What are 'best practice' approaches to detect intrusions? Monitor firewall logs? Monitor user activity?
    - Technology: Is the technology's data library current? Are automatic updates enabled?

- Analysis
    - People: Are IT staff capable to do the analysis required? Can they determine false positive activity?
    - Process: What is the process leadership wants to get effective and actionable data from IT staff? What are the demands for immediate and final reporting timelines?
    - Technology: Are the right tools on-site? Can open source/web solutions useful? Can DOD or DHS provide helpful data feeds to remain current of threats?

- Containment
    - People: Can IT staff stop the ongoing attack? Do they require additional coding scripting skills to build/update firewall policies?
    - Process: Is the containment process effective? Is allowing the attack to continue to identify the threat entity/location a good idea (to support law enforcement)?
    - Technology: Can software tools quarantine and stop a malware attack? Is shutting down all external connections a good immediate solution (at the firewall)?

- Recovery Actions
    - People: Can the IT staff recover backup data files and media?
    - Process: What is the order of recovery? Bring up internal databases and communications first and external servers (email and web site) be reestablished later? What are the recovery time standards for the company to regain business operations? What is acceptable? What is not acceptable?
    - Technology: Are there adequate numbers of back up devices for critical systems? Can third-party service providers assist in recovering lost or damaged data?

- User Response Activities
    - People: Can employees safely return to an operational state?
    - Process: Does the company need to control access to services to select individuals first (e.g., finance, logistics, etc.)

o Technology: Can technology resolve immediate problems from the recovery vice the employee such as, for example, reselecting printers and other data connections?

FULLY COMPLIANT: In those situations when control is specifically discussing a policy solution, the employment of automated tools, alerts, etc., should always be considered. Even the use of basic tracking tools such as Microsoft ® Excel ® and Access ® will at least demonstrate a level of positive control over the IT environment.

3.6.2 Track, document, and report incidents to appropriate officials and/or authorities both internal and external to the organization.

COMPLIANT: This control discusses the reporting requirements based on the severity of the incident as described above the DOD's Precedence Categorization diagram above. Ensure some form of the repository is maintained that an auditor could review at any time. Another reminder is that such information should be secured and encrypted at least at the CUI/CDI level.

FULLY COMPLIANT: A more complete response may include a dedicated computer server repository that could be physically disconnected from the system when not needed. This could prevent unauthorized access if an intruder is attempting to conduct intelligence collection or **reconnaissance** of the system; this would deny intruders critical network information and add confusion for their penetration activities.

Derived Security Requirements:

3.6.3 Test the organizational incident response capability.

COMPLIANT: Test the IR Plan at least annually. This should include both internal and external notional penetration exercises. These may include compromised login information and passwords provided to designated IT personnel. Ensure the results of the test are documented, reviewed, and signed by senior management. An IR test event should be maintained for any future audit.

FULLY COMPLIANT: This is not a requirement of this control and poses many risks to the IT environment. Do not recommend this solution; this would only be required based on the sensitivity of data, and Penetration Testing (PENTEST) is directed by the government. It is only offered for more of an appreciation of the complexity that a PENTEST entails.

A more expensive solution is hiring an outside Penetration Testing (PENTEST) company. Ensure that Rules of Engagement (ROE) are well established. Rules that should be affirmed by both the company and the PENTESTER, for example

, is that no inadvertent change or destruction of data is authorized. The PENTEST company may also require a liability release for any unintentional damage caused by the PENTEST. Always coordinate with legal professionals experienced in such matters to avoid any damage or confusion created by unclear expectations of a PENTEST.

MAINTENANCE (MA)
How do you take care of IT?

The MA security is relatively easy to address with regards to the requirements of NIST 800-171. This control requires processes and procedures that provide oversight of third-party vendors that offer IT maintenance and support. While this may appear vaguely paranoid, the company is required to exercise control of all maintenance personnel that potentially will have access to the company's and government's resident CUI/CDI and data. This will also typically require company escorts whose background have been properly checked and authorized to oversee outside workers.

Lack of maintenance or a failure to perform maintenance can result in the unauthorized disclosure of CUI/CDI. The full implementation of this requirement is contingent on the finalization of the proposed CUI/CDI federal regulation and marking guidance in the **CUI Registry**. (The marking requirements have been completed, and it is best to refer to the Registry, https://www.archives.gov/cui/registry/category-list, for specified industry codes.) These markings should be applied to business CUI/CDI data as well as IT hardware such as servers, desktops, laptops, etc.

Basic Security Requirements:

3.7.1 Perform maintenance on organizational information systems.
COMPLIANT: This should describe the company's maintenance procedures for its IT infrastructure. This could include either internal maintenance teams or third-party companies. This will include hardware component repairs and replacements, printer repairs, etc. Any maintenance agreements should be provided as artifacts to support an authorization package.

FULLY COMPLIANT: Maintenance could include the identification of computer hardware spares on-site or at company warehouse locations. Operational spares should be managed by the company's logistics' personnel; they should be captured within the property book database and its associated hard copy reporting to senior management.

3.7.2 Provide effective controls on the tools, techniques, mechanisms, and personnel used to conduct information system maintenance.
COMPLIANT: This control relates to tools used for diagnostics and repairs of the company's IT system/network. These tools include, for example, hardware/software diagnostic test equipment and hardware/software **packet sniffers**. Access to the hardware tools should be secured in lockable containers, and only accessed by authorized IT personnel.

In the case of software tools, they should be restricted to personnel with privileged user rights and specifically audited when any use is required or needed.

FULLY COMPLIANT: Suggested additional control may include two-person integrity requirements. This would require that when any of these types of tools are utilized, there should be at least two authorized individuals involved in any system maintenance or diagnostic activities.

Derived Security Requirements:

3.7.3 Ensure equipment removed for off-site maintenance is sanitized of any CUI.

COMPLIANT: Company data should be backed-up locally and secured for a future reinstall on another storage device or on the returned/repaired IT component. Also, the data should specifically be "wiped" by an industry-standard application for data deletion. There are many software tools that conduct multiple "passes" of data wipes to ensure sanitization of the media.

FULLY COMPLIANT: Any reports produced by the data "wiping" program could be captured in an equipment data log to provide proof of the action. Maintaining a hard copy of soft copy spreadsheet or database log would be helpful. Future inspections by the government may check this procedure to confirm the continuous application and repeatability of this procedure.

3.7.4 Check media containing diagnostic and test programs for malicious code before the media are used in the information system.

COMPLIANT: The normal solution for this is to conduct a scan using corporate anti-virus software applications.

FULLY COMPLIANT: A more thorough solution would include the use of an anti-malware application. Anti-malware programs are more comprehensive and proactively monitor **endpoints**, i.e., computers, laptops, servers, etc. (Anti-virus is not always designed to identify and clean malware, adware, worms, etc., from infected storage devices).

3.7.5 Require multifactor authentication to establish nonlocal maintenance sessions via external network connections and terminate such connections when nonlocal maintenance is complete.

COMPLIANT: Nonlocal maintenance are those diagnostic or repair activities conducted over network communications to include the Internet or dedicated least circuits.

This requires that any external third-party maintenance activities use some form of Multi-Factor Authentication (MFA) to directly access company IT hardware and software components. If IT personnel, working with outside maintainers can use an MFA solution then the company most likely has a robust IT support capability. If not, then this control is a good candidate for an early POAM; ensure good milestones are established for monthly review, for example, "on-going research," "market survey of potential candidate solutions," "identification of funding sources," etc.

FULLY COMPLIANT: A more complete answer requires a technical solution. As discussed earlier, the use of CAC, PIV cards, or tokens, such as the RSA ® rotating encryption keying devices are ideal solutions. This solution most likely will require additional analysis and funding approaches to select the most appropriate answer.

RSA Token (R)

3.7.6 Supervise the maintenance activities of maintenance personnel without required access authorization.

COMPLIANT: The procedure requirement should reflect that non-company maintenance personnel should always be escorted. An access log should be maintained, and it should include, for example, the individual or individuals, the represented company, the equipment repaired/diagnosed, the arrival and departure times, and the assigned escort. Maintain this hard-copy of soft-copy logs for future auditing purposes.

FULLY COMPLIANT: Procedural enhancements could include confirmed background checks of third-party maintainers and picture identification compared with the on-site individual. These additional enhancements should be based upon the sensitivity of the company's data. Any unattended CUI/CDI data should always be secured by CUI/CDI procedures—in a lockable container.

MEDIA PROTECTION (MP)
Create, protect, and destroy

The MP control was written to handle the challenges of managing and protecting the computer media storing CUI/CDI. This would include the governments' concerns about removable hard drives and especially the ability for a threat employ the use of a Universal Serial Bus (USB) "thumb drive."

> **Special Topic: DOD USB Policy**
>
> A UNIVERSAL SERIAL BUS (USB) OR **THUMB DRIVE** WHILE PROVIDING GREAT FLEXIBILITY TO MOVE DATA TO AND FROM SYSTEM DATA STORES, THEY ARE ALSO MAJOR MEANS TO INJECT MALICIOUS SOFTWARE SUCH AS VIRUSES AND RANSOMWARE INTO A COMPANY'S SECURITY BOUNDARY. DOD PROHIBITS USB USE IN DOD ENVIRONMENTS. IT'S CRITICAL TO ADDRESS THE PROPER CARE AND USE OF THESE IN A COMPANY'S IT INFRASTRUCTURE AND ASSOCIATED PROCEDURE GUIDE.

While most computer users are aware of the convenience of the thumb drive to help store, transfer, and maintain data, it is also a well-known threat vector where criminals and foreign threats can introduce serious malware and viruses into unsuspecting users' computers; the DOD forbids their use except under very specific and controlled instances.

MP is also about assurances by the business that proper destruction and sanitization of old storage devices has occurred. There are many instances where federal agencies have not implemented an effective sanitization process, and inadvertent disclosure of national security data has been released to the public. Cases include salvage companies discovering hard drives and disposed computers containing CUI/CDI and, in several cases, national security classified information, has occurred.

Be especially mindful that the sanitization process requires high-grade industry or government-approved applications that completely and effectively destroys all data on the target drive. Other processes may include physical shredding of the drive or destruction methods that further prevent the reconstruction of any virtual data by unauthorized personnel.

Basic Security Requirements:

3.8.1 Protect (i.e., physically control and securely store) information system media containing CUI, both paper and digital.

COMPLIANT: To implement this control the business should establish procedures regarding both CUI/CDI physical and virtual (disk drives) media. This should include only authorized personnel having access to individual and corporate sensitive data with requisite background checks and training. A business can use the foundations of other control families to further **mitigate** or reduce risks/threats.

RISK MANAGEMENT'S FOUNDATION:

MITIGATE OR REDUCE,

NOT ELIMINATION

OF THE RISK OR THREAT

A company can use other controls such as *more* training, longer audit log retention, *more* guards, or *more* complex passwords to **mitigate** any control. This would more clearly demonstrate to the government that the firm has a positive implementation of these security controls.

The use of other mitigating controls within NIST 800-171 are specifically about **risk reduction.** Any effort to use other families of controls to meet a specific control improves the overall IT infrastructure's security posture and is highly recommended.

FULLY COMPLIANT: The MP control can be further demonstrated by safeguarding physical files in secure or fire-resistant vaults. This could also include requirements for only IT personnel issuing property hand receipts for computer equipment or devices; a good accountability system is important.

3.8.2 Limit access to CUI on information system media to authorized users.

COMPLIANT: Identify in policy documents who, by name, title or function, has access to specified CUI/CDI. Any artifacts should include the policy document and an associated by-name roster of personnel assigned access by-system, e.g., accounting system, ordering system, patent repository, medical records, etc.

FULLY COMPLIANT: A more complete response could include logging of authorized personnel and providing a print-out of accesses over a one-month period.

3.8.3 Sanitize or destroy information system media containing CUI before disposal or release for reuse.

COMPLIANT: A good policy description is a must regarding data destruction of sensitive information within the government. Either use a commercial-grade "wiping" program, or physically destroy the drive.

If the company is either planning to internally reuse or sell to outside repurposing companies, ensure that the wiping is commercial grade or approved by the government. There are companies providing disk shredding or destruction services. Provide any service agreements that should specify the type and level of data destruction to government assessors.

NIST Special Publication 800-161

Supply Chain Risk Management
Practices for Federal Information
Systems and Organizations

FULLY COMPLIANT: For any assessment, the media sanitization company should provide **destruction certificates**. Chose several selected destruction certificates to include in the BOE submission. Typically, logistics and supply ordering sections of the business should manage as part of the Supply Chain Risk Management (SCRM) process.

A QUICK SIDE DISCUSSION ON SUPPLY CHAIN RISK MANAGEMENT

SCRM is a relatively new concern within the federal government. It is part of securing IT products within the business.

Questions that should be considered include:

- Is this product produced by the US or by an Ally?
- Could counterfeit IT items be purchased from less-than reputable entities?
- Is this IT product from an approved hardware/software product listing?

Users innately trust software developers to provide secure updates for their software applications and products that would add new functionalities or fix security vulnerabilities. They would not expect updates to be infected with malicious scripts, codes or programming. Most users have no mechanisms (or no concerns) about defending against seemingly legitimate software that is properly signed. Unfortunately, software unwittingly accessed by users and tainted by either nation-state actors or general cyber-criminals on the Internet pose an alarming risk to the global IT supply chain.

The use of varied supply chain attacks by cyber attackers to access corporate software development infrastructures have been major vectors of concerns for the government as well as private sector. These attacks typically include targeting publicly connected software build, test, update servers, and other portions of a software company's software development environment. Nation-state agents can then inject malware into software updates and releases have far-ranging impacts to the IT supply chain; the challenge continues to grow.[4]

Users become infected through official software distribution channels that are trusted. Attackers can add their malware to the development infrastructure of software vendors before they are compiled[5], hence, the malware is signed with the digital identity of a legitimate software vendor. This exploit bypasses typical "whitelisting" security measures making it difficult to identify the intrusion. This has contributed to a high degree of success by malicious cyber threat actors. Some example recent intrusions include:

- In July 2017, Chinese cyber espionage operatives changed the software packages of a legitimate software vendor, NetSarang Computer (https://www.netsarang.com/). These changes allowed access to a broad range of industries and institutions that included retail locations, financial services, transportation, telecommunications, energy, media, and academic.

- In August 2017, hackers inserted a backdoor into updates of the computer "cleanup" program, **CCleaner** while it was in its software development phases.

- In June 2017, suspected Russian actors **deployed the** PETYA ransomware to a wide-range of European targets by compromising a targeted Ukrainian software vendor

Another recent example of a supply chain compromise occurred in 2017. During this incident, Dell **lost** control of a customer support website and its associated Internet web address. Control of the website was wrested from a Dell support contractor that had failed to renew its authorized domain license and fees. The site was designed specifically to assist customers in the restoration of their computer and its data when infected. There were subsequent signs that the domain may have been infecting customers; two weeks after the contractor lost control of the address, the server that hosted the domain began appearing in numerous malware alerts.

The site was purchased by **TeamInternet.com,** a German company that specializes in Uniform Resource Locator (URL) **hijacking** and typosquatting[6] type exploits. (This company could also sell or lease the domain to anyone at that point to include back to Dell). They took advantage of

---

[4] Other less-protected portions of the supply chain include, for example, Field Programmable Gate Arrays (FPGA) and Application-Specific Integrated Circuit (ASIC) chips found on most major US weapons and satellite systems.

[5] Before they are converted as an executable (.exe) that are injected at the programming level where quality control mechanisms are often less-than adequate in secure development processes

[6] **Typosquatting** is a form of Uniform Resource Locator (URL) hijacking, and can be described as a form of cybersquatting and possibly brandjacking (e.g., Pepsie.com). It relies on mistakes by the individual especially due to "typos." It causes redirects using subtle and common variations in spellings to both malicious and marketing (adware) sites.

users believing they were going to a legitimate site and then being redirected to this redesigned malware site.

Supply chain compromises have been seen for years, but they have been mostly isolated and covert[7] in nature. They may follow with subsequent intrusions into targets of interest much later and provide a means for general hacking and damage to the company targets. The use of such a compromise provides highly likely means to support nation-state cyberespionage activities including those identified from Chinese IT equipment product builders. These include such companies such Chinese-based companies to include ZTE, Lenovo, and Huawei.

This trend continues to grow as there are more points in the supply chain that the attackers can penetrate using advance techniques. The techniques involved have become publicly discussed enough, and their proven usefulness encourages others to use these vectors of attack specific to damage and reconnaissance of governments, businesses and agencies globally. Advanced actors will likely continue to leverage this activity to conduct cyber espionage, cybercrime, and disruption. The dangers to the supply chain is of growing concern as the threat and risk landscapes continue to increase for the foreseeable future.

For further information see NIST 800-161, *Supply Chain Risk Management Practices for Federal Information Systems and Organizations.*
(http://nvlpubs.nist.gov/nistpubs/SpecialPublications/NIST.SP.800-161.pdf).

Derived Security Requirements:

3.8.4 Mark media with necessary CUI markings and distribution limitations.

COMPLIANT: This includes the marking of both physical documents as well as soft-copy versions. The best way to answer this is by referencing the following National Archives and Record Administration (NARA) document as part of the company's procedural guide that addresses this control:

- *Marking Controlled Unclassified Information*, Version 1.1 – December 6, 2016. (https://www.archives.gov/files/cui/20161206-cui-marking-handbook-v1-1.pdf)

EXAMPLE PROCEDURE: All company personnel will mark CUI/CDI, physical and virtual data, in accordance with the National Archives and Record Administration (NARA), Marking Controlled Unclassified Information, Version 1.1 – December 6, 2016. If there are questions

---

[7] Disclosing such information by a business may have both legal and reputation impacts; current US law under the 2015 Computer Information Security Act (CISA) does allow for "safe harbor" protections in the US.

about marking requirements, employees will refer these questions to their immediate supervisor or the corporate CUI/CDI officer."

FULLY COMPLIANT: This could include a screen capture that shows a government representative that onscreen access to CUI/CDI data is properly marked. A firm could also assign a CUI/CDI marking specialist; this person should be an individual with prior security experience and familiar with marking requirements. For example, this individual could additionally provide quarterly "brown bag" sessions where the "CUI/CDI Security Officer" provides training during lunchtime sessions. Be creative when considering more thorough means to reinforce cybersecurity control requirements.

3.8.5 Control access to media containing CUI and maintain accountability for media during transport outside of controlled areas.

COMPLIANT: This control is about "transport outside of controlled areas." This too is a matter of only authorized individuals (couriers) be authorized by position, training, and security checks that should be considered when the company needs to transport CUI/CDI external to its typical corporate location.

Individuals should be provided either courier cards or orders that are signed by an authorized company representative typically responsible for oversight of security matters. This could be, for example, the corporate security officer, Information System Security Manager (ISSM), or their designated representative. These individuals should be readily known to other employees and managers who have demanded to move CUI/CDI to outside locations. This would demonstrate there is available and on-call personnel based on the business mission and priorities. This also should be a limited cadre of personnel that management relies on for such external courier services.

FULLY COMPLIANT: The company could hire an outside contract service that transports both physical and computer media containing CUI/CDI based on the company's mission.

3.8.6 Implement cryptographic mechanisms to protect the confidentiality of CUI stored on digital media during transport unless otherwise protected by alternative physical safeguards.

COMPLIANT: This is a Data at Rest (DAR) issue. See Control 3.1.3 for depiction. The recommendation is that all CUI/CDI needs to be encrypted. A common application that has been used is BitLocker ®. It provides password protection to "lock down" any transportable media. It is not the only solution, and there are many solutions that can be used to secure DAR.

The 256-bit key length is the common standard for commercial and government encryption applications for hard drives, removable drives, and even USB devices. The government requires

DAR must always be encrypted; it is best to resource and research acceptable tools that the government supports and recognizes.

FULLY COMPLIANT: The reinforcing of this control may include using enhanced physical security measures. This could include hardened and lockable carry cases. Only authorized employees should transport designated CUI/CDI. This should also be captured in the submitted BOE.

3.8.7 Control the use of removable media on information system components.

COMPLIANT: Identify in corporate policy the types and kinds of removable media that can be attached to fixed desktop and laptop computers. These could include external hard drives, optical drives, or USB thumb drives.

Strongly recommend that thumb drives are not used; if needed, then designate IT security personnel who can authorize their restricted use. This should also include anti-virus/malware scans before their use.

FULLY COMPLIANT: Removeable media drives can be "blocked" by changes in system **registry** settings; company IT personnel should be able to prevent such designated devices from accessing the computer and accessing the company network.

3.8.8 Prohibit the use of portable storage devices when such devices have no identifiable owner.

COMPLIANT: This should be established in the company procedure. If such devices are found, they should be surrendered to security, and scanned immediately for any viruses, malware, etc.

FULLY COMPLIANT: As described in Control 3.8.7, IT personnel can block unauthorized devices from attaching to the computer/network by updating registry settings.

3.8.9 Protect the confidentiality of backup CUI at storage locations.

COMPLIANT: *This is a Data at Rest (DAR) issue.* See Control 3.1.3 for a depiction. See Control 3.8.6 for suggested requirements for the protection of CUI/CDI under a DAR solution.

FULLY COMPLIANT: See Control 3.8.6 for additional means to protect CUI/CDI.

PERSONNEL SECURITY (PS)
Background Checks

This is a relatively simple control. It most likely is already implemented within the company and only requires procedural documents are provided in the submission. This should include both civil and criminal background checks using a reputable company that can process the individual background checks through the Federal Bureau of Investigation (FBI). Background Checking companies can also do other forms of personnel checks to include individual social media presence or financial solvency matters that may avoid any future embarrassment for the company.

While these checks are not well defined for company's under NIST 800-171, it should meet minimum government standards for a **Public Trust** review. Discuss with the Contract Officer what the requirements they suggest be met to provide the level of background check required to meet the NIST 800-171 requirement. Also, it is always best to work with HR and legal experts when formulating a personnel security policy to include the types and kinds of investigations are in accordance with applicable state and federal law in this area.

Basic Security Requirements:

3.9.1 Screen individuals prior to authorizing access to information systems containing CUI.

COMPLIANT: This control requires some form of background check be conducted for employees. There are number of firms that can provide criminal and civil background checks based upon individual's personal information and their fingerprints.

The company should capture its HR process regarding background checks in the company cybersecurity procedure document. It's also important to address when a reinvestigation is required. The suggestion is at least every 3 years or upon recognition by managers of potential legal occurrences that may include financial problems, domestic violence, etc. This control should be highly integrated with the company HR and legal policies.

FULLY COMPLIANT: Some background companies can, for an additional fee, conduct active monitoring of individuals when major personal or financial changes occur in a person's life. Update company procedural guides with all details of the company's established process.

3.9.2 Ensure that CUI and information systems containing CUI are protected during and after personnel actions such as terminations and transfers.

COMPLIANT: This control is about procedures regarding whether termination is amicable or not. Always have clear terms about non-removal of corporate data and CUI/CDI after departure from the company to include databases, customer listings, and proprietary data/IP. This should include legal implications for violation of the policy.

FULLY COMPLIANT: The technical solution could include monitoring by IT staff of all account activity during the out-processing period. This could also include immediate account lock-outs on the departure date. Also recommend that there are changes to all vault combinations, building accesses, etc., that the individual had specific access to during their tenure.

Derived Security Requirements: None.

PHYSICAL PROTECTION (PP)
Guards and moats....

Physical security is part of a company's overall protection of its people and facilities. A little-known fact is that the guiding principle for any *true* cybersecurity professional is to protect the life and safety of the people supported. This control is also about the protection of damage to corporate assets, facilities, or equipment; this includes any loss or destruction of the material computer equipment secured by the PP security control. This controls addresses the physical security that also includes such elements as guards, alarm systems, cameras, etc., that help the company protect its sensitive company data and, of course, its NIST 800-171 CUI.

There are no limits on how to harden a company's "castle walls," but for any owner, the cost is always a major consideration. Protecting vital CUI/CDI while seemingly expansive under this control allows for reasonable flexibility. Again, the company should reasonably define its success under the NIST 800-171 controls. "Success" can be defined from the company's point of view regarding complexity or cost but must be prepared to defend any proposed solution to government assessors.

Basic Security Requirements:

3.10.1 Limit physical access to organizational information systems, equipment, and the respective operating environments to authorized individuals.
COMPLIANT: Of importance for this control, is limiting access to corporate data servers, backup devices, and specifically, the "computer farm." If the company is maintaining devices on its premises, then policy should address who has authorized access to such sensitive areas.

If the corporation is using an off-site **Cloud Service Provider (CSP)**, capture in part or full sections of any CSP service agreements specific to physical security measures. Both types of computer architectures should address for example areas of interest such as access logs, after-hours access, camera monitoring, unauthorized access reporting criteria, types and kinds of network defense devices such as Intrusion Detection and Prevention Systems (IDS/IPS), etc., as part of the corporate procedure.

FULLY COMPLIANT: This could include active alerting to both management and security personnel that includes phone calls, email alerts, or SMS text messages to designated company security personnel. Security measures and **alert thresholds** should be driven by the sensitivity of the data stored. Management should make **risk-based** determinations of the cost and returns on effectiveness to drive the corporate policy for this control as well as other solutions.

3.10.2 Protect and monitor the physical facility and support infrastructure for those information systems.

COMPLIANT/FULLY COMPLIANT: This control can be addressed in many ways by physical security measures. This should include locked doors, cipher locks, safes, security cameras, guard forces, etc. This control should be answered by the current physical protections that prevent direct entry into the company and physical access to its IT devices and networks.

Derived Security Requirements:

3.10.3 Escort visitors and monitor visitor activity.

COMPLIANT: Much as described under the MA control above, like security measures as described in Control 3.7.6 should be employed.

FULLY COMPLIANT: Also, refer to Control 3.7.6 on greater security measures that can be used to demonstrate more complete compliance with this control.

3.10.4 Maintain audit logs of physical access.

COMPLIANT /FULLY COMPLIANT: Refer to Control 3.7.6 for suggested audit log items. This should address personnel during operating and after hour entry into the company and its IT facilities. This should include logs specific to outside third-party vendors and subcontractors; any such procedures should also apply to those individuals who are not direct employees.

3.10.5 Control and manage physical access devices.

COMPLIANT: This control requires that physical access devices such as security badges, combinations, and physical keys are managed through both procedure and logs (physical or automated). The company needs to demonstrate to the government its positive security measures to protect its CUI/CDI data. While this control may appear easier than the technical policy control settings used by the company for its IT systems, it is no less important.

FULLY COMPLIANT: If not already in place, identify and separate the physical security functions (e.g., facility security officer, etc.) from the technical security functions managed by corporate IT personnel with the requisite skills and experiences. Companies should avoid duty-creep on its cybersecurity personnel and define roles and responsibilities between its classic security functions (e.g., physical, personnel security, etc.) and the roles and responsibilities of its cyber workforce that may reduce their effectiveness of both security areas.

Cybersecurity workforce duty-creep is a real-world occurrence; Companies are unwittingly shifting overall "security" functions from classic security personnel to cybersecurity professionals creating security gaps for a company or agency

3.10.6 Enforce safeguarding measures for CUI at alternate work sites (e.g., telework sites).

COMPLIANT: (See Control 3.1.3 for the explanation of DAR and DIT). This control can be easily addressed by DAR application solutions. Laptops should always be password protected; this should be part of any central cybersecurity policy document and enforced by technical solutions deployed by company IT personnel. Additionally, The DIT protections are afforded by corporate VPN and 2FA/MFA solutions.

FULLY COMPLIANT: The company should establish minimum requirements for telework protection. This could include, for example, work should be conducted in a physically securable area, the VPN should always be used, corporate assets should not use unsecured networks such as at coffee shops, fast-food restaurants, etc. This could also include an explicit telework agreement for employees before being authorized telework permission, and it should be closely coordinated with HR and legal experts.

RISK ASSESSMENT (RA)
Dealing with Changes to the Infrastructure

This is an important chapter for contract offices. If there are "security relevant" changes that happen within the software, hardware, and/or IT environment architecture, the contract office should be notified of the changes specific to these controls.

A "security relevant" change while probably unlikely to happen may most likely take the form of architectural changes more specifically in the area of "cloud computing." Treat cloud computing as a third-party, managed service, that is also contracted to provide some or many of the NIST 800-171 controls. This should take the form of a contract between the business or a Service Level Agreement (SLA) in addition to such a contract. Ensure those artifacts are provided to the contract office's packet specific to the target company.

The RA control relies on a continual process to determine whether changes in hardware, software or architecture create either a major positive or negative **security-relevant** effect. This is typically done by using a **Change Request** (CR). If an upgrade to, for example, the Window 10 ® Secure Host Baseline Operating System software, and it improves the security posture of the network, a Risk Assessment (RA) is needed and associated **risk analysis** should be performed by authorized technical personnel. This could take the form of a technical report that management accepts from its IT staff for approval or disapproval of the change. Management, working with its IT staff, should determine thresholds when a formal RA activity needs to occur.

The RA process affords a great amount of flexibility during the life of the system and should be used when other-than, for example, a new application or **security patches** are applied. Security patches' updates are typically integrated into Operating Systems and applications. IT personnel should regularly also manually check for normal functional and security patch updates from the software companies' websites.

"Negative" security-relevant effects on the corporate IT infrastructure include, for example, a major re-architecture event or a move to a Cloud Service Provider. While these events may not seem "negative," NIST standards require a full reassessment. In other words, plan accordingly if the company is going to embark on a major overhaul of its IT system. There will be a need under these circumstances to consider the impacts to the company's current Authority to Operate (ATO). These types of event typically necessitate that the NIST 800-171 process is redone; prior work in terms of policies and procedures can be reused to receive an updated ATO.

The decision-tree below is designed to help a company determine when to consider an RA:

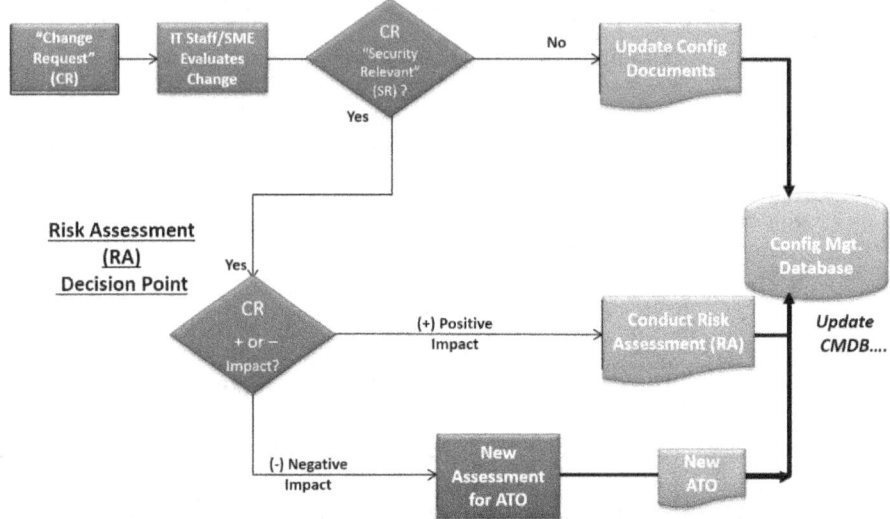

Decision-tree Addressing Risk Assessment & "Security Relevance"[8]

<u>**Basic Security Requirements:**</u>

3.11.1 Periodically assess the risk to organizational operations (including mission, functions, image, or reputation), organizational assets, and individuals, resulting from the operation of organizational information systems and the associated processing, storage, or transmission of CUI.

COMPLIANT: RA's are required when there is a "major" change due to either a hardware change (e.g., replacing an old firewall with a new Cisco ® firewall), software version upgrades (e.g., moving from Adobe ® 8.0 to 9.0), or changes to architecture (e.g., adding a new backup drive). The consideration is always about *how* this change to the baseline configuration is either a positive (normal) or negative (preferably, highly unlikely)?

It is important to describe the corporate RA process in terms of change needed and overall risk to the IT system. This should include who conducts the technical portion of the RA and who, in senior management, for example, the Chief Operating Officer (COO) or Chief Information Officer (CIO) that determines final approval.

---

[8] This decision-tree is based upon the overall impact of the change to the IT environment. Where the change is positive a RA is only recommended, and where there is a negative impact, then a full ATO effort must be reinitiated.

This is as new to Federal Contracting as it is to the company; understand there will be "growing pains," as the government continues to better define its procedures

While not thoroughly discussed as part of this book, *the integration of the NIST 800-171 with federal government contracting is in its infancy*. It is best to coordinate and advise the government Contract Officers of any changes. It is always "best practice" to maintain a history of RA development and approval for future auditing.

FULLY COMPLIANT: Implementing a more defined RA process could include standardized formats for RA artifacts. This could include a technical report written by knowledgeable IT personnel about a change, or a simplified form that allows for a checklist-like approach. It could also employ an outside third-party company that would formalize a review of the changes and their analysis of the overall impact to system security.

Derived Security Requirements:

3.11.2 Scan for vulnerabilities in the information system and applications periodically and when new vulnerabilities affecting the system are identified.

COMPLIANT: This control requires that the company (system owner) regularly scans for vulnerabilities in the information system and hosted applications based upon a defined frequency or randomly based upon an established policy or procedure. This is also supposed to be applied when new vulnerabilities affecting the system or applications are identified.

The simplest way to address this control is using **anti-virus** and **anti-malware** enterprise-levels of software versions. Major players in these areas include Symantec ®, McAfee ®, and

> **Reminder**
>
> **Supply Chain Risk Management (SCRM)**
>
> The Russian-based software developer, Kaspersky Lab's ® Anti-virus solutions are currently prohibited.

Malwarebytes ®. Procedural documents should describe the products used to address "new vulnerabilities" using these solutions. See also SYSTEM AND INFORMATION INTEGRITY (SI) as a reinforcing control for this RA control.

FULLY COMPLIANT: A suggested more complete implementation could be the leveraging of company ISP services also is identified for providing a secondary layer of defense as a form of "trusted" connection. This could include any available SLA's that define the service provider's ability to mitigate such additional threats by employing **whitelisting** and **blacklisting** services; these services are designed to allow or restrict access depending on an **Access Control List** (ACL). See Control 3.14.2 for a more detailed description.

3.11.3 Remediate vulnerabilities in accordance with assessments of risk.

COMPLIANT: Typically, anti-virus and anti-malware security applications cannot only detect but remove and quarantine malicious software. Update documentation accordingly.

This control also addresses "vulnerabilities" that are created by not meeting a specific control within the identified NIST 800-171 families. To address these re-assessment activities, it is normal to update system POAM documentation with explicit reasons any control is not met in full. This should attempt to answer what mitigation solutions are employed? When, by a specific date, the vulnerability will be corrected?

FULLY COMPLIANT: Some additional means to better address this RA control is through other external services that can support ongoing remediation efforts. This could include the company's ISP or Cloud Service Providers. This could also include regular reviews of POAMs by both management and IT support staff personnel, for example, monthly or quarterly.

SECURITY ASSESSMENT (SA)
Beginning Continuous Monitoring and Control Reviews

The SA control is about a process that re-assesses the state of all security controls and whether changes have occurred requiring additional mitigations of new risks or threats. The standard is 1/3rd of the controls are to be re-assessed annually. This would require designated IT personnel conduct a SA event of approximately 36-37 controls per year. This should be captured in what is called a **ConMon Plan**.

Continuous Monitoring is a key component of the NIST 800 series cybersecurity protection framework. It is defined as "...maintaining ongoing awareness of information security, vulnerabilities, and threats to support organizational risk management decisions," (NIST Special Publication 800-137, *Information Security Continuous Monitoring (ISCM) for Federal Information Systems and Organizations*, http://nvlpubs.nist.gov/nistpubs/Legacy/SP/nistspecialpublication800-137.pdf).

ConMon is a significant guiding principle for the recurring execution of a Security Assessment

---

Basic Security Requirements:

3.12.1 Periodically assess the security controls in organizational information systems to determine if the controls are effective in their application.
COMPLIANT: As described in the opening paragraph, meeting the basic requirements of the Security Assessment control should include the creation of a ConMon Plan and a review of 33% of the controls at least annually.

FULLY COMPLIANT: A more thorough execution could include more than 33% of the controls being reviewed and reassessed; it is suggested to provide the results of annual Security Assessments to government contracting or their designated recipients.

3.12.2 Develop and implement plans of action designed to correct deficiencies and reduce or eliminate vulnerabilities in organizational information systems.

COMPLIANT: Where the security control is not fully implemented by the company or not recognized by the government as being fully compliant, a detailed POAM is necessary; review guidance under the AC control for a more detailed discussion of what is required in preparing a POAM for review.

As described earlier, this should include activities that are meant to answer the control in full or at least leverage other physical and virtual elements of other security controls to reinforce the posture of the control in question. A well-written POAM that is tracked and managed serves as the foundation for a strong risk management process.

> **Cybersecurity is a leadership, not a technical challenge**

FULLY COMPLIANT: Regular reviews by management and IT staff should enhance the company's cybersecurity posture. Cybersecurity is not just something that IT security personnel do; it includes the active oversight and review by corporate leadership to ensure effectiveness.

3.12.3 Monitor information system security controls on an ongoing basis to ensure the continued effectiveness of the controls.

COMPLIANT: This control can be answered in terms of a well-developed and executed ConMon Plan. Describing its purpose and the actions of assigned personnel to accomplish this task will answer this control.

FULLY COMPLIANT: Suggested additional efforts regarding this control could include ad hoc spot checks of controls outside of the annual review process. Identify using the **PPT Model** described in Control 3.6.1 who is responsible for conducting the assessment (people), the workflow to adequately assess the current state of the control (process), and any supporting automation that provides feedback and reporting to management (technology).

1.12.4 Develop, document, and periodically update system security plans that describe system boundaries, system environments of operation, how security requirements are implemented, and the relationships with or connections to other systems.

COMPLIANT: this control requires that the **SSP** is updated regularly. The SSP should at a minimum be reviewed *annually* by designated company cybersecurity/IT personnel to ensure its accuracy. The SSP should be specifically updated sooner if there are major changes to the:

- Hardware
- Software
- Network Architecture/Topology

FULLY COMPLIANT: A more complete means to address this control is by addressing in company change control boards. These are regular meetings when changes to hardware, software or architecture occur. This should include mechanisms to document the occurrence of application and security patching. An effective procedure should always address changes to the IT system.

Derived Security Requirements: None.

SYSTEM AND COMMUNICATIONS PROTECTION (SC)
External Communication and Connection Security

The overall risk management strategy is a key in establishing the appropriate technical solutions as well as procedural direction and guidance for the company. The core of this security control is it establishes policy based upon applicable federal laws, Executive Orders, directives, regulations, policies, standards, and guidance. This control focuses on information security policy that can reflect the complexity of a business and its operation with the government. The procedures should be established for the security of the overall IT architecture and specifically for the components (hardware and software) of the information system.

In this control, many of the prior reinforcing controls can be used in demonstrating to the government a fuller understanding of NIST 800-171 requirements. The apparent repetition of other already developed technical solutions and procedural guides can be used as supporting these controls. However, it is important that corporate procedures are addressed individually—this is for traceability purposes of any potential current or future audit of the company's work by the government; clear and aligned explanations of the controls will make the approval process quicker.

Basic Security Requirements:

3.13.1 Monitor, control, and protect organizational communications (i.e., information transmitted or received by organizational information systems) at the external boundaries and key internal boundaries of the information systems.
COMPLIANT: This control can be answered in the corporate procedure and include, for example, active auditing that checks for unauthorized access, individuals (external) who have had numerous failed logons, and traffic entering the network from "blacklisted" addresses, etc. The company should refer to its specific audit procedure as described in more detail under the AU control.

FULLY COMPLIANT: This control could be better met as formerly discussed by using "smart" firewalls and advanced SIEM solutions. While costlier and requiring greater technical experience, corporate leadership should consider. These solutions while not necessarily cost effective for the current state of the company, it should be considered as part of any future architectural change effort. Any planning efforts should consider current and future technology purchases meant to enhance the cybersecurity posture of the company.

3.13.2 Employ architectural designs, software development techniques, and systems engineering principles that promote effective information security within organizational information systems.

MINIMUM/FULLY COMPLIANT: Describing effective security architectural design measures can be as simple as the employment of a properly configured firewall or 2FA/MFA utilized by the company. It is highly likely that the average company seeking contracts with the government will be specifically concerned with basic and secure architectures.

Other **mitigation** elements that can be described for this control may include physical security measures (e.g., a 24-hour guard force, reinforced fire doors, and cameras) or blacklist measures that prevent unauthorized applications from executing in the corporate network. See Control 3.13.10 for how 2FA operates internal or external to a company's network.

Derived Security Requirements:

3.13.3 Separate user functionality from information system management functionality.

COMPLIANT: The policy should not allow privileged users to use the same credentials to access their user (e.g., email and Internet searches) and privileged user accesses. This separation of access is a basic network security principle and is intended to hamper both insider and external threats. (A suggested review of a similar control is Control 3.1.4, and its discussion of the **segregation of duty** principle for comparison.)

FULLY COMPLIANT: There are technical solutions to automate this process. The product, for example, CyberArk ® is used in many parts of the federal government to track and account for privileged user activity that is easily auditable. The ability to oversee especially privileged user activity should be readily audited and reviewed by senior company cybersecurity representatives.

3.13.4 Prevent unauthorized and unintended information transfer via shared system resources.

COMPLIANT: **Peer-to-peer** networking is not authorized within many parts of the government, and it is strongly suggested the corporation's network also forbids its use. This is typically part of the AUP and should be enforceable to prevent, e.g., insider threat opportunities or used by external hackers to gain unauthorized access using legitimate employee security credentials.

FULLY COMPLIANT: Suggest that this is part of the normal audit activity by designated IT personnel. They could be reviewing audit logs for unauthorized connections to include peer-to-peer networking.

3.13.5 Implement subnetworks for publicly accessible system components that are physically or logically separated from internal networks.

MINIMUM/FULLY COMPLIANT: The simplest answer is that subnetworks reduce an intruder's ability to effectively exploit corporate network addresses. Have IT personnel establish subnetworks specifically for the email and webservers that are in the external Demilitarized Zone (DMZ) of the corporate's security boundary; see Control 3.14.2 for the location of a DMZ relative to the company's network. Some companies maintain external database servers; ensure they too have established subnetwork addresses.

3.13.6 Deny network communications traffic by default and allow network communications traffic by exception (i.e., deny all, permit by exception).

COMPLIANT/FULLY COMPLIANT: Like Control 3.4.8, this control can be selected by IT personnel. This is a technical control that should also be captured in the procedure document. These network settings are typically set at the firewall and involve **whitelisting** (only permitting access by exception) and **blacklisting** (from non-authorized Internet addresses) everyone else to enter the network. (Also, review Control 3.14.2.)

3.13.7 Prevent remote devices from simultaneously establishing non-remote connections with the information system and communicating via some other connection to resources in external networks.

COMPLIANT/FULLY COMPLIANT: If a teleworking employee uses their remote device (i.e., notebook computer), and then connects to a non-remote (external) connection, it allows for an unauthorized external connection to exist; this provides a potential hacker with the ability to enter the network using the authorized employee's credentials.

It is critical that the company requires employees to use their VPN connection and blocks any unsecure connections from accessing internal systems or applications. IT personnel need to ensure these settings are properly configured and are part of the corporate cybersecurity procedure documentation.

3.13.8 Implement cryptographic mechanisms to prevent unauthorized disclosure of CUI during transmission unless otherwise protected by alternative physical safeguards.

COMPLIANT: Remember, this control is about external communications from the network and its system boundary. This is a DIT issue and is protected by the cryptographic solutions discussed earlier; see Control 3.1.3. Documentation should reflect the type and level of protection of data transmitted. Any additional protections such as a VPN, a secure circuit/dedicated circuit provided by a commercially contracted carrier may afford more security for company data transmissions.

FULLY COMPLIANT: Better levels of protection could be addressed regarding defense in depth which is a current operational philosophy supported by the government; additional layers of security provide additional defense. (See the "Defense-in-Depth" diagram at Control 3.14.2).

3.13.9 Terminate network connections associated with communications sessions at the end of the sessions or after a defined period of inactivity.

COMPLIANT: This was addressed in the AC control specific to the complete termination of a session. Sessions of suggested importance would be those such as to the financial, HR, or other key computer server systems housing defined CUI/CDI. It is recommended that the procedure is updated specifically to this control re-using language provided by any response to the control(s) discussing the termination of a network connection.

FULLY COMPLIANT: Audit of sessions that have timed-out can strengthen this control. SA's and IT staff can determine from audit logs that the prescribed time-out period was met and enforced. Provide a sampling to any inspector as part of the final packet.

3.13.10 Establish and manage cryptographic keys for cryptography employed in the information system.

COMPLIANT: There are two major scenarios likely to occur:

1. Use of commercial cryptographic programs that resides within the company's architecture or is provided by an external "managed service" provider are the most likely scenarios. The keys will be maintained and secured by the cryptographic application. The company is establishing some form of 2FA solution. The public key would be secured somewhere else in the architecture, and the private key, that of the employee, would reside on a token such as CAC card or another key device.

2. Using a 2FA solution with a CAC, Personal Identity Verification (PIV) card or "token" such as those produced by RSA ® is likely if the government authorizes the exchange of security keys on its systems with that of the company. This requires a Certificate Authority (CA) usually outside the local network either managed by the government or another trusted commercial entity with the capability to support "asymmetric" 2FA.

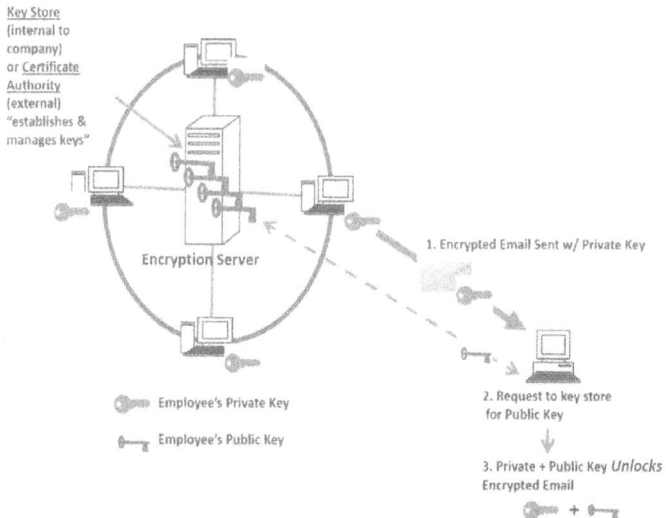

Two-factor Authentication (2FA) – Asymmetric Cryptography Basic Description

Whichever solution is used, ensure compatibility with government systems and other companies' as part of its normal operations. ***All transmittal of CUI/CDI data is required to be encrypted.***

FULLY COMPLIANT: Any greater ability to secure and protect the **key store** within the company or through defined SLA's with outside service providers is important. Ensure they have safeguards in place to protect unauthorized access to its system as well; they may use stronger encryption methods, but ensure they are recognized by the government and are Federal Information Processing Standards (FIPS 140-2) compliant. (See Control 3.13.11 for identifying FIPS 140-2 solutions).

3.13.11 Employ FIPS-validated cryptography when used to protect the confidentiality of CUI.

COMPLIANT /FULLY COMPLIANT: The company needs to confirm that its encryption applications are FIPS 140-2 compliant. It can easily be verified at the website below:

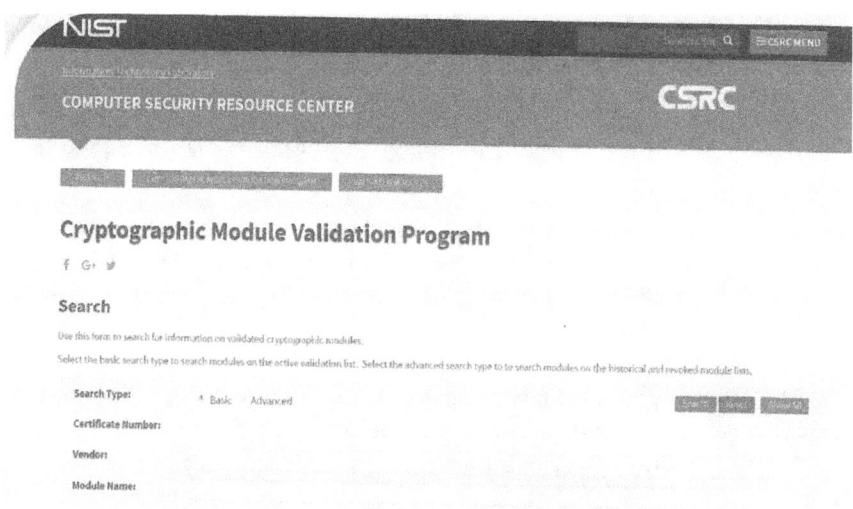

Official NIST site to confirm FIPS 140-2 cryptographic compliance
(https://csrc.nist.gov/projects/cryptographic-module-validation-program/validated-modules/search)

3.13.12 Prohibit remote activation of collaborative computing devices and provide indication of devices in use to users present at the device.

COMPLIANT: Collaborative computing devices include, for example, "networked whiteboards, cameras, and microphones." The intent is to prevent these devices being used by intruders to conduct reconnaissance of a network.

This can be prevented by changes in registry settings that only authorized IT personnel with privileged access can change. Furthermore, if these items are active, visible lighting or audible alerts, should be considered to notify IT and security personnel. Policy should require that individuals do not change these settings to include privileged users. Any change should only be approved by exception and require a privileged user who is authorized to make such changes.

FULLY COMPLIANT: Auditing and SIEM solutions could be configured to ensure these settings are not tampered with. See Control 3.3.2 for further discussion of this topic area.

3.13.13 Control and monitor the use of mobile code.

COMPLIANT /FULLY COMPLIANT: Mobile code is mainly part of Internet-capable business phones. The company's phone carrier can limit the types and kinds of mobile applications that reside on employee phones. Most applications are usually required to meet secure industry development standards. It is best to confirm with the company's carrier how mobile code apps are secured and restrict employees to a set number of approved mobile apps. Define in the company procedures the base applications provided to each employee, and the process for work specific applications that other specialists in the company require.

3.13.14 Control and monitor the use of Voice over Internet Protocol (VoIP) technologies.

COMPLIANT: The most likely current place VOIP would exist is the company's phone service. Ensure with the phone carrier that their VOIP services are secure and what level of security is used to protect corporate communications. Furthermore, identify any contract information that provides details about the provided security.

FULLY COMPLIANT: Verify what monitoring services and network protection (from malware, viruses, etc.) are part of the current service plan. If necessary, determine whether both the control and monitoring are included or extra services. If not fully included, consider formulating a POAM.

3.13.15 Protect the authenticity of communications sessions.

COMPLIANT / FULLY COMPLIANT: This control addresses communications' protection and establishes confidence that the session is authentic; it ensures the identity of the individual and the information being transmitted. Authenticity protection includes, for example, protecting against session hijacking or insertion of false information.

This can be resolved by some form, hard or soft token MFA/2FA, solution. It will ensure the identity and FIPS 140-2 encryption to prevent data manipulation. See Control 3.5.2 for further discussion. While these are not absolute solutions, they greatly demonstrate more certainty that the communications are authentic.

3.13.16 Protect the confidentiality of CUI at rest.

COMPLIANT: This is a DAR issue, and as discussed earlier, it is a government requirement. Ensure the proper software package is procured that meets FIPS 140-2 standards. (See Control 3.13.11 for NIST's website information).

FULLY COMPLIANT: If using a CSP, ensure it is using government accepted FIPS 140-2 standards; it will make authorization simpler. And, a reminder, if the business cannot use FIPS 140-2 solutions, ensures an effective POAM is developed that addresses why it cannot be currently implemented and when the company is prepared to implement the control. *When will the company be compliant?*

SYSTEM AND INFORMATION INTEGRITY (SI)
Anti-virus and Anti-Malware

This control family is about maintaining the integrity of data within the company's system security boundary. It primarily defended by active measures such as anti-virus and malware protection. This control addresses the establishment of procedures for effective implementation of the security controls. Cybersecurity policies and procedures may include Information Security (INFOSEC) policies. Company risk management strategy is a key factor in establishing decisive system protections.

Basic Security Requirements:

3.14.1 Identify, report, and correct information and information system flaws in a timely manner.

COMPLIANT: This control addresses what are considered security-relevant flaws. These would include, for example, software patches, hotfixes, anti-virus and anti-malware signatures.

Typically, network Operating Systems can check with manufacturers via the Internet for updated, e.g., "security patches" in near-real time. It is important to allow patches from the authorized manufacturers and sources be updated as soon as possible. They usually are designed to fix bugs and minor through major security vulnerabilities. The sooner the system is updated, the better. Ensure a process, such as checks by IT personnel at least twice a day. Many systems will allow for automated "pushes" to the network. Ensure that documented processes account for review by IT personnel to "audit" known pushes by only authorized sources.

Major Security Events/Zero-Day Attacks: There are times that the federal government becomes aware of **zero-day attacks**. These are attacks where there is no current security patch and sometimes requires other actions by government supported organizations and corporations; be aware of these events from DOD and Department of Homeland Security (DHS) alerts. These will require near-immediate action. Furthermore, the government may direct everyone, including NIST 800-171 authorized businesses, report their status to the Contract Officer by an established deadline.

FULLY COMPLIANT: Ensure that designated IT personnel are aware of and are monitoring the active vulnerabilities sites from both DOD and DHS. An active process to verify the current state of threats against the government is an excellent means to establish a company's due diligence in this area.

DHS's United States Computer Emergency Readiness Team (US-CERT) has the latest information on vulnerabilities to include zero-day updates. It is also recommended that designated IT personnel sign up for the Rich Site Summary (RSS) data feeds by the selecting the symbol to the left. The address for the overall site is: https://www.us-cert.gov/ncas/current-activity

3.14.2 Provide protection from malicious code at appropriate locations within organizational information systems.

COMPLIANT: Protecting the network from malicious code is typically through both active anti-virus and malware protection applications or services. Ensure if additional protections provided by the businesses' commercial ISP are included in any artifact submission.

FULLY COMPLIANT: Any additional protections could be provided by "smart" firewalls, routers, and switches. Certain commercial devices provide extra defenses.

Smart Firewalls. Smart firewalls include standard protection capabilities. Additionally, firewalls specifically, can afford whitelisting and blacklisting protections.

- **Whitelisting** can be used only to allow authorized outside users on an internal Access Control List (ACL). The ACL needs to be managed actively to ensure that legitimate organizations can communicate through the businesses' firewall. The external interested business or organizations can still communicate with the business for some services like the company web site and email system that resides in what is termed the Demilitarized Zone (DMZ). Whitelisting is typically implemented at the firewall. See Diagram below.

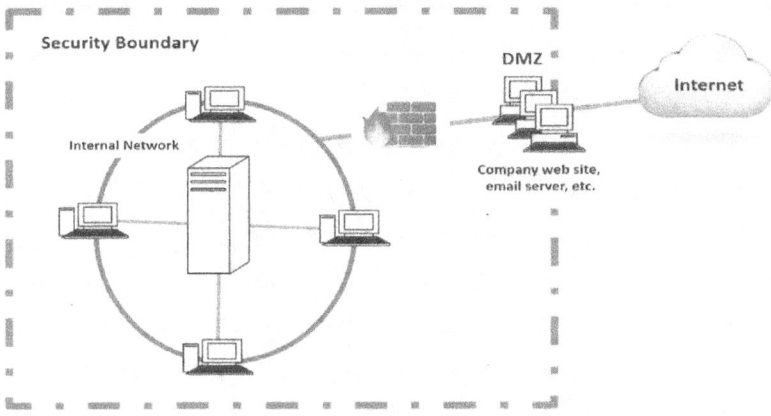

Basic Company Network View

- **Blacklisting** is used to block known "bad guys." There are companies and the government that can provide lists of known malicious sites based upon their Internet address. Blacklists require continuous management to be most effective.

Both solutions are not guaranteed. While they afford additional means to slow hackers and nation-state intruders, they are not total solutions. Therefore, the government, and much of the cybersecurity community, strongly supports the principle of **defense in depth** where other technological solutions help to reinforce the protections because of security programming flaws inadvertently created by software developers and the constant challenge of hackers exploiting various areas of modern IT architectures to conduct their nefarious actions.

The Principle of Defense in Depth

3.14.3 Monitor information system security alerts and advisories and take appropriate actions in response.

COMPLIANT: This SI control can be best met through auditing. This can be met by using applications (such as anti-virus) or tools embedded within the architecture. These should include Intrusion Detection capabilities, network packet capture tools such as Wireshark ®, or audit logs. The process and associated actions should include recognition and notification to senior management. Management should ensure developed processes define when an event is raised to a level of a notifiable incident to the government.

FULLY COMPLIANT: A more-complete solution could use other advanced toolsets based on the education and experience of the IT support staff. These could include malicious code protection software (such as found in more advanced anti-malware solutions). Consideration should always include the overall ROI for the investment in such tools.

If the company can only implement minor portions of the control and has the planned intent to invest in improved tools in the future, it is best to develop a well-defined POAM with achievable milestones for the company to pursue. It will demonstrate to the US government a commitment to improving cybersecurity vice ignoring other technical methods to reduce the risk to the company and its associated CUI/CDI.

Derived Security Requirements:

3.14.4 Update malicious code protection mechanisms when new releases are available.

COMPLIANT /COMPLETE ANSWER: This is usually easily resolved through ongoing software license agreements with vendors for malicious code internal programs or external contracted support services. Assuming a new version is made available during the active period of the license, updates are typically free; document the company's procedure for maintaining not only current but legal versions of malicious code detection and prevention software or services.

3.14.5 Perform periodic scans of the information system and real-time scans of files from external sources as files are downloaded, opened, or executed.

COMPLIANT: Many of the solutions already discussed afford real-time scanning of files and traffic as they traverse the network. Scanning of files should always be conducted from external downloads for both viruses and malware. Ensure the technical policy settings are always set to conduct real-time scans of the network, endpoints (i.e., work computers both internal and used by teleworking employees), and files entering the network by the appropriate tools to ensure network operation and security.

FULLY COMPLIANT: Require IT personnel to regularly check that real-time scanning has not been changed accidentally or on purpose. It is important to be aware that potential intruders will attempt to shut down any security features such as active scanning. Train IT personnel to manually check at least weekly and alert management if the changes are suspicious. Identifying possible entry into the company's data is a function of the SI as well as a major component of the AU control family.

3.14.6 Monitor the information system including inbound and outbound communications traffic, to detect attacks and indicators of potential attacks.

COMPLIANT: As discussed, anti-virus and malware provide some level of checking of inbound and outbound traffic. Document both manual and automated means to ensure traffic is monitored.

Procedures should identify the people who will conduct the regular review, the process that ensures proper oversight is in place to identify violations of this control, and what technologies are being used to protect inbound and outbound traffic from attack. (See Control 3.6.1 for discussion about the PPT Model, and its application to address security controls).

FULLY COMPLIANT: This could also identify commercial ISP's supporting the business with "trusted" connections to the Internet. Refer to provided SLA's and contract information for government review.

3.14.7 Identify unauthorized use of the information system.

COMPLIANT: This is met through active and regular auditing of, for example, systems, applications, intrusion detections, and firewall logs. It is important to recognize that there may be limitations for the IT staff to properly and adequately review all available logs created by the company's IT network. It is best to identify the critical logs to review regularly and any secondary logs as time permits. Avoid trying to review all available system logs; there are many. Also, determine the level of effort, required processing time, ability, and training of the company's' IT support staff.

FULLY COMPLIANT: In addition to the above, consider third-party companies that can provide a monitoring service of the network. While these may be expensive, it will depend on the business, its mission, and the critically of the data. This solution will require a well-developed SLA's with appropriate oversight to ensure the company receives the Quality of Service (QOS) the company needs.

Conclusion
This is Risk Management, NOT Risk Elimination

The major premise of the NIST cybersecurity process is to recognize that it's not about the absolute certainty that the security controls will stop every type of cyber-attack. The role that the contract professional generates is the initial assurances that the company has met the required BOE and support artifacts to establish a level of due diligence that the contractor has attempted a "good faith" effort to protect federal data—and, its own. Risk Management is about recognizing the system's overall weaknesses. It's about the company's leadership, not just the IT staff, has identified where those weaknesses exist.

Risk Management is also about a defined Continuous Monitoring (ConMon) and effective Risk Assessment processes. Such processes afford the needed protection to a company's sensitive CUI/CDI. These are not meant to be complete answers to an ever-changing risk landscape. It is only through an active and continual review of the controls can the government or companies ensure near-certainty their networks are as secure *as possible.*

NIST 800-171 is becoming the national cybersecurity standard between federal government operations and its huge contractor support workforce in the very near future. A main objective of this book is to provide a plain-English and how-to guide for the non-IT Contract Professionals and their support staff. The target of this book is to provide information on how to best assess and verify the 110 NIST 800-171 designated controls are "adequately" met. It provides a constructive starting point for contract professionals to not only meet the requirements of NIST 800-171, but to truly protect Government, to include CUI, and in the case DOD, CDI data from modification, exfiltration or destruction. It's more importantly about protecting these national IT systems and their data from the "bad guys."

APPENDIX A – Relevant References

Federal Information Security Modernization Act of 2014 (P.L. 113-283), December 2014.
http://www.gpo.gov/fdsys/pkg/PLAW-113publ283/pdf/PLAW-113publ283.pdf

Executive Order 13556, *Controlled Unclassified Information*, November 2010.
http://www.gpo.gov/fdsys/pkg/FR-2010-11-09/pdf/2010-28360.pdf

Executive Order 13636, *Improving Critical Infrastructure Cybersecurity*, February 2013.
http://www.gpo.gov/fdsys/pkg/FR-2013-02-19/pdf/2013-03915.pdf

National Institute of Standards and Technology Federal Information Processing Standards Publication 200 (as amended), *Minimum Security Requirements for Federal Information and Information Systems*.
http://csrc.nist.gov/publications/fips/fips200/FIPS-200-final-march.pdf

National Institute of Standards and Technology Special Publication 800-53 (as amended), *Security and Privacy Controls for Federal Information Systems and Organizations*.
http://dx.doi.org/10.6028/NIST.SP.800-53r4

National Institute of Standards and Technology Special Publication 800-171, rev. 1, *Protecting Controlled Unclassified Information in Nonfederal Information Systems and Organizations*.
https://nvlpubs.nist.gov/nistpubs/SpecialPublications/NIST.SP.800-171r1.pdf

National Institute of Standards and Technology Special Publication 800-171A, *Assessing Security Requirements for Controlled Unclassified Information*
https://csrc.nist.gov/CSRC/media/Publications/sp/800-171a/draft/sp800-171A-draft.pdf

National Institute of Standards and Technology *Framework for Improving Critical Infrastructure Cybersecurity* (as amended).
http://www.nist.gov/cyberframework

APPENDIX B – Relevant Terms & Glossary

Audit log.
A chronological record of information system activities, including records of system accesses and operations performed in a given period.

Authentication.
Verifying the identity of a user, process, or device, often as a prerequisite to allowing access to resources in an information system.

Availability.
Ensuring timely and reliable access to and use of information.

Baseline Configuration.
A documented set of specifications for an information system, or a configuration item within a system, that has been formally reviewed and agreed on at a given point in time, and which can be changed only through change control procedures.

Blacklisting.
The process used to identify: (i) software programs that are not authorized to execute on an information system; or (ii) prohibited websites.

Confidentiality.
Preserving authorized restrictions on information access and disclosure, including means for protecting personal privacy and proprietary information.

Configuration Management.
 A collection of activities focused on establishing and maintaining the integrity of information technology products and information systems, through control of processes for initializing, changing, and monitoring the configurations of those products and systems throughout the system development life cycle.

Controlled Unclassified Information (CUI/CDI).

Information that law, regulation, or governmentwide policy requires to have safeguarding or disseminating controls, excluding information that is classified under Executive Order 13526, Classified National Security Information, December 29, 2009, or any predecessor or successor order, or the Atomic Energy Act of 1954, as amended.

External network.
A network not controlled by the company.

FIPS-validated cryptography.
A cryptographic module validated by the Cryptographic Module Validation Program (CMVP) to meet requirements specified in FIPS Publication 140-2 (as amended). As a prerequisite to CMVP validation, the cryptographic module is required to employ a cryptographic algorithm implementation that has successfully passed validation

testing by the Cryptographic Algorithm Validation Program (CAVP).

Hardware. The physical components of an information system.

Incident. An occurrence that actually or potentially jeopardizes the confidentiality, integrity, or availability of an information system or the information the system processes, stores, or transmits or that constitutes a violation or imminent threat of violation of security policies, security procedures, or acceptable use policies.

Information Security. The protection of information and information systems from unauthorized access, use, disclosure, disruption, modification, or destruction to provide confidentiality, integrity, and availability.

Information System. A discrete set of information resources organized for the collection, processing, maintenance, use, sharing, dissemination, or disposition of information.

Information Technology. Any equipment or interconnected system or subsystem of equipment that is used in the automatic acquisition, storage, manipulation, management, movement, control, display, switching, interchange, transmission, or reception of data or information by the executive agency. It includes computers, ancillary equipment, software, firmware, and similar procedures, services (including support services), and related resources.

Integrity. Guarding against improper information modification or destruction and includes ensuring information non-repudiation and authenticity.

Internal Network. A network where: (i) the establishment, maintenance, and provisioning of security controls are under the direct control of organizational employees or contractors; or (ii) cryptographic encapsulation or similar security technology implemented between organization-controlled endpoints, provides the same effect (at least with regard to confidentiality and integrity).

Malicious Code. Software intended to perform an unauthorized process that will have adverse impact on the confidentiality, integrity, or availability of an information system. A virus, worm, Trojan horse, or other code-based entity that infects a host. Spyware and some forms of adware are also examples of malicious code.

Media. Physical devices or writing surfaces including, but not limited to, magnetic tapes, optical disks, magnetic disks, and printouts (but not including display media) onto which information is recorded, stored, or printed within an information system.

Mobile Code. Software programs or parts of programs obtained from remote information systems, transmitted across a network, and executed on a local information system without explicit installation or execution by the recipient.

Mobile device. A portable computing device that: (i) has a small form factor such that it can easily be carried by a single individual; (ii) is designed to operate without a physical connection (e.g., wirelessly transmit or receive information); (iii) possesses local, nonremovable or removable data storage; and (iv) includes a self-contained power source. Mobile devices may also include voice communication capabilities, on-board sensors that allow the devices to capture information, and/or built-in features for synchronizing local data with remote locations. Examples include smartphones, tablets, and E-readers.

Multifactor Authentication. Authentication using two or more different factors to achieve authentication. Factors include: (i) something you know (e.g., password/PIN); (ii) something you have (e.g., cryptographic identification device, token); or (iii) something you are (e.g., biometric).

Nonfederal Information System. An information system that does not meet the criteria for a federal information system. nonfederal organization.

Network. Information system(s) implemented with a collection of interconnected components. Such components may include routers, hubs, cabling, telecommunications controllers, key distribution centers, and technical control devices.

Portable storage device. An information system component that can be inserted into and removed from an information system, and that is used to store data or information (e.g., text, video, audio, and/or image data). Such components are typically implemented on magnetic, optical, or solid state devices (e.g., floppy disks, compact/digital video disks, flash/thumb drives, external hard disk drives, and flash memory cards/drives that contain nonvolatile memory).

Privileged Account. An information system account with authorizations of a privileged user.

Privileged User. A user that is authorized (and therefore, trusted) to perform security-relevant functions that ordinary users are not authorized to perform.

Remote Access. Access to an organizational information system by a user (or a process acting on behalf of a user) communicating through an external network (e.g., the Internet).

Risk.
A measure of the extent to which an entity is threatened by a potential circumstance or event, and typically a function of: (i) the adverse impacts that would arise if the circumstance or event occurs; and (ii) the likelihood of occurrence. Information system-related security risks are those risks that arise from the loss of confidentiality, integrity, or availability of information or information systems and reflect the potential adverse impacts to organizational operations (including mission, functions, image, or reputation), organizational assets, individuals, other organizations, and the Nation.

Sanitization.
Actions taken to render data written on media unrecoverable by both ordinary and, for some forms of sanitization, extraordinary means. Process to remove information from media such that data recovery is not possible. It includes removing all classified labels, markings, and activity logs.

Security Control.
A safeguard or countermeasure prescribed for an information system or an organization designed to protect the confidentiality, integrity, and availability of its information and to meet a set of defined security requirements.

Security Control Assessment.
The testing or evaluation of security controls to determine the extent to which the controls are implemented correctly, operating as intended, and producing the desired outcome with respect to meeting the security requirements for an information system or organization.

Security Functions.
The hardware, software, and/or firmware of the information system responsible for enforcing the system security policy and supporting the isolation of code and data on which the protection is based.

Threat.
Any circumstance or event with the potential to adversely impact organizational operations (including mission, functions, image, or reputation), organizational assets, individuals, other organizations, or the Nation through an information system via unauthorized access, destruction, disclosure, modification of information, and/or denial of service.

Whitelisting.
The process used to identify: (i) software programs that are authorized to execute on an information system.

APPENDIX C – Managing the Lifecycle of a POAM

Intelligence Cycle Approach for the POAM Lifecycle

This section is designed to provide a structure for anyone developing a POAM for their company or agency. It describes how to approach the POAM development process and how to easily formulate and track POAMs during their lifecycle. We suggest using the US Intelligence Community's *Intelligence Lifecycle* as a guide to address POAM's from "cradle-to-grave." The process has been slightly modified to provide a more pertinent description for the purposes of POAM creation, but we have found this model to be effective for the novice through professional cybersecurity or IT specialist that works regularly in this arena.

This includes the following six stages:

1. **IDENTIFY:** Those controls that time, technology or cost that cannot be met to satisfy the unimplemented control.

2. **RESEARCH:** You now have decided the control is not going to meet your immediate NIST 800-171 needs. The typical initial milestone is to conduct some form of research or market survey of available solutions. This will include:

    - **The kind or type of solution.** Either as a person (e.g., additional expertise), process (e.g., what established workflow can provide a repeatable solution) or technology (e.g. what hardware/software solution fixes all or part of the control.
    - **How the federal government wants it implemented**? For example, are hard tokens required or can the company use some form of soft token solution to address 2FA?
    - **Internal challenges.** What does the company face overall with people, process, or technology perspectives specific to the control?

3. **RECOMMEND:** At this phase, all research and analysis has been done, and presumably well-documented. Typically, the cybersecurity team or business IT team will formulate recommended solutions to the System Owner, i.e., the business decision-makers such as the Chief Information or Operations Officer. The recommendations must not only be technically feasible, but cost and resources should be part of any recommendation.

4. **DECIDE:** At this point, company decision-makers not only approve of the approach to correct the security shortfall but have agreed to resourcing requirements to authorize the expenditures of funds and efforts.

5. **IMPLEMENT:** Finally, the solution is implemented, and the POAM is updated for closure. This should be reported to the Contract Office or its representative on a recurring basis.

6. **CONTINUAL IMPROVEMENT.** Like any process, it should be regularly reviewed and updated specific to the needs and capabilities of the company or organization. This could include better templates, additional staffing, or more regular updates to management to ensure both a thorough but supportive understanding of how cybersecurity meets the needs and mission of the business.

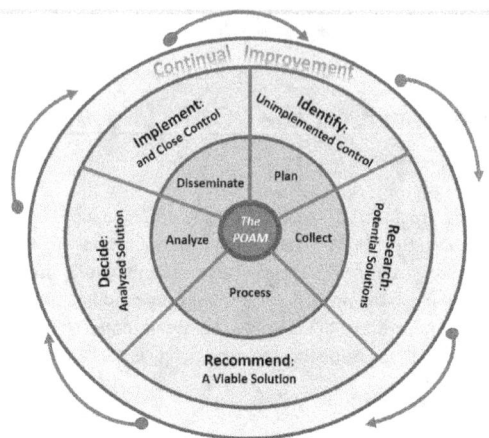

The POAM Lifecycle

We begin in the "Identify" section of the lifecycle process above. At this stage several things may occur. Either the business owner or IT staff recognizes that the security control is not or cannot be immediately met, or they employ an automated security tool, such as ACAS® or Nessus®, that identifies securities vulnerabilities within the IS. This could also include findings such as the default password, like "password," has not been changed on an internal switch or router. It could also include updated security patching has not occurred; some automated applications will not only identify but recommend courses of action to mitigate or fix a security finding. Always try to leverage those as soon as possible to secure your IT environment.

Also, assumed in this stage is the act of documenting findings. The finding should be placed in a POAM template as the business moves through the lifecycle. This could be done using documents created in Word®, for example, but recommend using a spreadsheet program that allows the easier filtering and management of the POAM. Spreadsheets afford greater flexibility during the "heavy lift" portion of formulating all POAM's not intended to be fixed immediately because of technical shortfalls. This would include not having in-house technical expertise, for example, to setup Two Factor Authentication (2FA) or because of current company financial limitations; this would most likely be reasonable when the costs are currently prohibitive to implement a specific control.

In the "research" phase this includes technical analysis, Internet searches, market research, etc., regarding viable solutions to address the security control not being "compliant." This activity is typically part of initial milestone established in the POAM. It may be added in the POAM, and could be, for example: "Conduct an initial market research of candidate systems that can provide an affordable Two Factor Authentication (2FA) solution to meet security control 3.X.X." Another example might be: "The cybersecurity section will identify at least two candidate Data at Rest (DAR) solutions to protect the company's corporate and CUI data." These initial milestones are a normal part of any initial milestones that clearly describes reasonable actions to address non-complaint controls.

Another part of any milestone establishment action is to identify when a milestone is expected to be complete. Typically, milestones are done for a 30-day period, but if the complexity of such an activity requires additional time, ensure the company as identified reasonable periods of times with actual dates of *expected* completion. Never use undefined milestones such as "next version update" or "Calendar Year 2020 in Quarter 4." Real dates are mandatory to truly manage findings supported by, for example, automated workflow or tracking applications the company may acquire in the future to enhance its cybersecurity risk management program.

At the "recommendation" phase, this is the time when the prior research has resulted in at least one solution, be it additional skilled personnel (people), enhanced company policies that manage the security control better (process), or a device that solves the control in part or total (technology). This should be part of this phase and be part of the POAM template as a milestone with the expected completion date.

At the "decide" phase, company or agency decision-makers should approve a recommended solution and that decision should be documented in a configuration change tracking document, configuration management decision memorandum or in the POAM itself. This should include approved resources, but most importantly, any funding decision should be acted upon as quickly as possible. While many of these suggestions may seem basic, it is often overlooked to document the decision so future personnel and management can understand how the solution was determined.

The "implementation" phase may become the most difficult. It is where a lead should be designated to coordinate the specific activity to meet the control— it may not necessarily be a technical solution, but may also include, for example, a documentation development activity that creates a process to manage the POAM.

Implementation should also include basic programmatic considerations. This should include performance, schedule, cost, and risk:

- Performance: consider what success the solution is attempting to address. Will it can send email alerts to users? Will the system shutdown automatically once an intrusion is confirmed in the corporate network? Will the Incident Response Plan include notifications to law enforcement? Performance is always a significant and measurable means to ensure that the solution will address the POAM/security control shortfall. Always try to measure performance specific to the actual control that is being met.

- Schedule: Devise a plan based upon the developed milestones that are reasonable and not unrealistic. As soon as a deviation becomes apparent, ensure that the POAM template is updated and approved by management. This should be a senior management representative with the authority to provide extensions to the current plan. This could include, for example, a Senior IT Manager, Chief Information Security Officer, or Chief Operating Officer.

- Cost: While it is assumed all funding has been provided early in the process, always ensure contingencies are in place to request additional funding. It is common in most IT programs to maintain a 15-20% funding reserve for emergencies. Otherwise, the Project Manager or lead will have to re-justify to management for additional funding late in the implementation portion of the cycle.

- Risk: This is not the risk identified, for example, by the review of security controls or automated scans of the system. This risk is specific to the program's success to accomplish its goal to close the security finding. Risk should always in particular focus on the performance, cost, and schedule risks as major concerns. Consider creating a risk matrix or risk log to help during the implementation phase.

Finally, ensure that as soon as the company can satisfactorily implement its solution close the control and notify the Contract Office of the completion. Typically, updates and notifications should occur at least once a quarter, but more often is appropriate for more highly impactful controls. Two-factor authentication and automated auditing, for example, are best updated as quickly as possible. This not only secures the company's network and IT environment but builds confidence with the government that security requirements are being met.

A final area to consider in terms of best-practices within cybersecurity, and more specifically in developing complete POAMs, is the area of **continual improvement**. Leveraging the legacy Intelligence Lifecycle process should be an ongoing model for IT and cybersecurity specialists to emulate. Those supporting this process should always be prepared to make changes or modifications that better represent the state and readiness of the system with its listing of POAMs. The Intelligence Lifecycle provides the ideal model for a business to follow and implement to meet its POAM responsibilities within NIST 800-171.

APPENDIX D--Sample Cloud Service Level Agreement (CSLA) with Suggested Comments/Actions

1. Purpose and Scope

The Objective of this "Service Level Agreement" (hereinafter "SLA" for short) is to define the reference parameters for the provision of the [CLOUD SERVICE PROVIDER] service (hereinafter "Service" for short) and for monitoring the level of quality provided. The objective of the SLA is also to define the rules of interaction between [CSP] and the Customer. This SLA is an integral part of the Contract completed between [CSP] and the Customer with the rules defined in [OTHER GENERALIZED PROVISIONING DOCUMENTS, IF REQUIRED]. This SLA applies separately to each Customer and for each Contract.

2. Validity and Duration – Modifications and Replacements

This SLA shall enter into force for an indefinite period for each Customer after the conclusion of each Contract and shall end with the termination of the Contract to which it relates. [CSP] reserves the right to change or replace it several times [NOTE: CUSTOMER HAS AN OPPORTUNITY TO LIMIT CHANGES AND SHOULD ALSO REQUIRE AT LEAST A TWO_WEEK NOTICE OF PENDING CHANGES] during the Contract and at any time. Changes made to the SLA or the new SLA - replacement of the previous one - shall always enter into force for an indefinite [SHOULD ALWAYS BE NEGOTIABLE; LIMIT IT TO THE FULL TERM OF THE CONTRACT OR AT SPECIFICED OPTION PERIODS OF THE CONTRACT] period or until the next change or replacement, from the date of their publication on the page [CAN INCLUDE REFERENCE DOCUMENT OR PUBLIC CSP WEB PAGE FOR CHANGES IN THE TERM OF SERVICES]; However, in this case the Customer shall be given the opportunity to withdraw from the contract according to the rules defined in the contract [THIS SHOULD BE A SEPARATE DOCUMENT] within thirty days of the date of publication of the change and/or the replacement of the SLA. In the event of a withdrawal by the Customer the rules laid down in the Conditions of Service Provision applies.

3.   Operational Functionality

3.1. [CSP] will make every reasonable effort [REMEMBER: IF STANDARDS ARE NOT MET, THERE SHOULD BDE A FINANCIAL IMPACT TO THE CSP DEFINED IN THE MAIN CONTRACT] to ensure maximum availability of the virtual infrastructure created and allocated by the Customer and, at the same time, the observance of the following operational functionality parameters:

A) Resources of the Data Center via which the Service is provided:

- 100% uptime on an annual basis for electricity and/or air conditioning;
- The switching off the virtual infrastructure created and allocated by the Customer caused by a general lack of the power supply and/or air conditioning is a malfunction for which, based on its duration, by way of compensation the Customer will be due credit [ENSURE THIS AREA IS REVIEWED BY LEGAL REPRESENTATIVES] determined in accordance with [CONTRACT, OR OTHER SUPPORT DOCUMENT] of this SLA;
- 99.95% uptime on an annual basis and accessibility via the Internet to the virtual infrastructure created and allocated by the Customer;
- The complete inaccessibility via the Internet to the virtual infrastructure created and allocated by the Customer for a total time longer than that determined by the Uptime guaranteed parameter by [CSP] is a malfunction for which, based on its duration, by way of compensation the Customer will be due credit according to [DEFINED DOCUMENT] of this SLA.

B) Virtual infrastructure created and allocated by the Customer:
- 99.95% uptime on an annual basis, for the availability of physical nodes (servers) hosting the virtual infrastructure;
- The failure of the virtual infrastructure created and allocated by the Customer - for a total time longer than that determined by the Uptime guaranteed parameter by [CSP] - caused by failures and/or anomalies of the physical nodes is a malfunction for which, based on its duration, by way of compensation the Customer will be due credit according to [DEFINED DOCUMENT] of this SLA.

3.2. If the Customer purchases the [EXTENDED SUPPORT] via [CONTRACT/SLA MECHANISM], [CSP] will make every reasonable effort to ensure maximum availability of the virtual infrastructure created and allocated by the Customer and, at the same time, the observance of the following operational function parameters:

A) Resources of the Data Center through which the Service is provided:
- 100% uptime on an annual basis for power supply and/or air conditioning;
- The switching off the virtual infrastructure created and allocated by the Customer caused by a general lack of power supply and/or air conditioning is a malfunction which, based on its duration, entitles the Customer, by way of compensation, to the credit established in accordance with [DEFINED DOCUMENT] of this SLA;
- 99.8% uptime on an annual basis, of accessibility via the internet to the virtual infrastructure created and allocated by the Customer;
- The complete inaccessibility via the Internet to the virtual infrastructure created and allocated by the Customer for a total amount of time longer than the amount of time determined by the Uptime parameter guaranteed by [CSP] is a malfunction which, based on its duration, entitles the Customer, by way of compensation, to the credit

established in accordance with [DEFINED DOCUMENT] of this SLA.

B) Virtual infrastructure created and allocated by the Customer:
- 99.8% uptime on an annual basis, for the availability of physical nodes (servers) hosting the virtual infrastructure;
- Failure of the virtual infrastructure created and allocated by the Customer - for a total amount of time longer than the amount of time determined by the Uptime parameter guaranteed by [CSP] - caused by failures and/or anomalies of the physical nodes is a malfunction which, based on its duration, entitles the Customer, by way of compensation, to the credit established in accordance with [DEFINED DOCUMENT] of this SLA.

4. Planned Maintenance

4.1. Time for planned maintenance is not counted in the Uptime calculation. Planned maintenance concerns activities regularly carried out by [CSP] to maintain the functionality of the Data Center resources by means of which the Service and the physical nodes that host the virtual infrastructure is provided; both ordinary and extraordinary.

4.2. The implementation of the maintenance [GENERAL MAINTENANCE ONLY; THIS SHOULD BE DEFINED BY CSP] operations will be communicated to the Customer by [CSP] with at least 48 hours' notice by email sent to the email address indicated in the order phase. [CSP] is committed to making every reasonable effort to carry out the planned maintenance tasks at times with minimal impact to the Customer's virtual infrastructure.

5. Detecting Failures and Faults

5.1. Any failures and/or faults of the resources of the Data Center by means of which the Service or the physical nodes that host the virtual infrastructure created and allocated by the Customer is provided, shall be reported by the Customer by opening a ticket on the service page [DEFINED LOCATION OR MECHANISM REQUIRED]; for the purposes of awarding credits, however, only malfunctions also confirmed by [CSP; THERE NEEDS TO BE A DISPUTE MECHANISM SUCH AS ARBITRATION THAT IS DEFINED IN THE MAIN CONTRACT BY LEGAL PROFESSIONALS] monitoring system will be taken into consideration.

5.2. Failures or faults can be reported by the Customer to the [CSP] support service 24 hours a day. Any reports received will be promptly forwarded to the technical support strictly respecting the chronological order of receipt.

5.3. Monitoring by [CSP] is carried out using specific software packages that detect and indicate any failures or faults by notifying the support service which operates 24/7, 365 days a year in real-time.

6.   Refunds and Credits

6.1. For the purposes of this SLA [CSP] awards the customer, by way of compensation, with credit equal to 5% [NOTE: REFER THIS TO LEGAL FOR REVIEW] of the total expenditure generated - in thirty days prior to the malfunction or rather in the month previous to the month affected by the malfunction if the Customer has purchased a Service with a monthly plan (such as, by way of example only, [EXTENDED CLOUD SERVICES]) - by the virtual infrastructure concerned by it for each complete portion of fifteen minutes of malfunction beyond the limits set by this SLA, up to a maximum of three (300) hundred minutes[SUGGEST LEGAL REVIEW BASED UPON THE SERVICE TYPE SUPPORTED].

6.2. To be awarded the credit the Customer must contact the [CSP] Support Service by opening a ticket on the website [OR OTHER DEFINED MECHANISM] within 30 days from the end of the Malfunction. Credits awarded by [CSP] will only be issued by crediting the amount to [SPECIFIED COMPANY ACCOUNT OR OTHER DEFINED MEANS TO ACCEPT CREDITS FOR DOWN-TIME ISSUES].

6.3. Notwithstanding the above, it remains in any case understood that during the period of its inactivity, the Service is not generating expense and therefore for this period the corresponding amount provided in the Price List for each of the resources created and allocated by the Customer in the virtual infrastructure will not be deducted from the Top-up; any amount deducted by mistake will be reimbursed by [CSP].

6.4. The Customer agrees and accepts that in case of purchase of a Service with a monthly plan (such as, by way of example only, [EXTENDED SERVICE PLAN], he/she shall not be entitled to any refund from [CSP] for the period of Service inactivity except for the credit referred to in the paragraph 6.1.

7. Applicability Limits

Listed below are the conditions in the presence of which, despite the occurrence of any malfunction, the Customer is not due any compensation provided by the SLA:

- Due to a Force Majeure, i.e. events that, objectively, would prevent [CSP] staff from intervening to perform the tasks set out by the Contract which are [CSP] responsibility (merely by way of example and not exhaustive: strikes and demonstrations which block communication routes; road accidents; wars and acts of terrorism, natural disasters such as flooding, storms, hurricanes, etc.);
- Extraordinary interventions to be carried out urgently at the sole discretion of [CSP] to avoid hazards to safety and/or stability and/or confidentiality and/or integrity of the virtual

infrastructure created and allocated by the Customer and the data and/or information contained therein. Any execution of these measures will be communicated to the Customer via email sent to the email address provided when ordering with less than 48 hours' notice, or at the start of the operations in question or in any case, as soon as possible;

- Unavailability or blocks of the virtual infrastructure created and allocated by the Customer due to:

1. Incorrect use, incorrect configuration or shut-down commands voluntarily or involuntarily performed by the customer;
2. Faults and malfunctions of application/management software provided by third parties;
3. Non-fulfilment or breach of Contract due to the Customer;

- Fault or malfunction of the Service, or their failure or delayed removal or elimination due to non-fulfilment or breach of Contract by the Customer or to an abuse of the Service by the Customer;
- Failure by the virtual infrastructure to connect to the public network voluntarily, or due to the Customer;
- Causes that lead to total or partial inaccessibility of the virtual infrastructure created and allocated by the Customer due to faults in the Internet network beyond [CSP's] perimeter, and therefore beyond its control (merely by way of example, failures or problems).

[SIGNATURE BLOCKS FOR AUTHORIZED REPRESENTATIVE FOR THE CSP TO ACCEPT TERMS OF CSLA]

[SIGNATURE BLOCKS FOR AUTHORIZED REPRESENTATIVE FOR THE CSC TO ACCEPT TERMS OF CSLA]

APPENDIX E – NIST 800-171 Compliance Checklist

The following compliance checklist is intended to provide a guide to conduct a "self-assessment" of the company's overall cybersecurity posture as required by NIST 800-171.

*Assessment Method: Refer to NIST 800-171A, **Assessing Security Requirements for Controlled Unclassified Information**, that describes types and means to self-validate the control. The three assessment methods are: examine, interview and test.

Control #	Description	Assessment Method*	Document (e.g., SSP or Co. Procedure Guide)	Page #	Reviewed By	Validated By
Access Control (AC)						
3.1.1	*Limit information system access to authorized users, processes acting on behalf of authorized users, or devices (including other information systems)*					
3.1.1[a]	*Authorized users are identified.*					
3.1.1[b]	*Processes acting on behalf of authorized users are identified.*					
3.1.1[c]	*Devices (and other systems) authorized to connect to the system are identified.*					
3.1.1[d]	*System access is limited to authorized users.*					
3.1.1[e]	*System access is limited to processes acting on behalf of authorized users.*					
3.1.1[f]	*System access is limited to authorized devices (including other systems).*					
3.1.1[a]	*Authorized users are identified.*					
3.1.2	*Limit information system access to the types of transactions and functions that authorized users are permitted to execute*					
3.1.2[a]	*The types of transactions and functions that authorized users are permitted to execute are defined.*					
3.1.2[b]	*System access is limited to the defined types of transactions and functions for authorized users.*					

3.1.3	Control the flow of CUI in accordance with approved authorizations	
3.1.3[a]	Information flow control policies are defined.	
3.1.3[b]	Methods and enforcement mechanisms for controlling the flow of CUI are defined.	
3.1.3[c]	Designated sources and destinations (e.g., networks, individuals, and devices) for CUI within the system and between interconnected systems are identified.	
3.1.3[d]	Authorizations for controlling the flow of CUI are defined.	
3.1.3[e]	Approved authorizations for controlling the flow of CUI are enforced.	
3.1.4	Separate the duties of individuals to reduce the risk of malevolent activity without collusion	
3.1.4[a]	The duties of individuals requiring separation are defined.	
3.1.4[b]	Responsibilities for duties that require separation are assigned to separate individuals.	
3.1.4[c]	Access privileges that enable individuals to exercise the duties that require separation are granted to separate individuals.	
3.1.5	Employ the principle of least privilege, including for specific security functions and privileged accounts	
3.1.5[a]	Privileged accounts are identified.	
3.1.5[b]	Access to privileged accounts is authorized in accordance with the principle of least privilege.	
3.1.5[c]	Security functions are identified.	
3.1.5[d]	Access to security functions is authorized in accordance with the principle of least privilege.	
3.1.6	Use non-privileged accounts or roles when accessing nonsecurity functions	
3.1.6[a]	Nonsecurity functions are identified.	
3.1.6[b]	Users are required to use non-privileged accounts or roles when accessing nonsecurity functions.	

3.1.7	**_Prevent non-privileged users from executing privileged functions and audit the execution of such functions_**
3.1.7[a]	_Privileged functions are defined._
3.1.7[b]	_Non-privileged users are defined._
3.1.7[c]	_Non-privileged users are prevented from executing privileged functions._
3.1.7[d]	_The execution of privileged functions is captured in audit logs._
3.1.8	**_Limit unsuccessful logon attempts_**
3.1.8[a]	_The means of limiting unsuccessful logon attempts is defined._
3.1.8[b]	_The defined means of limiting unsuccessful logon attempts is implemented._
3.1.9	**_Provide privacy and security notices consistent with applicable CUI rules_**
3.1.9[a]	_Privacy and security notices required by CUI-specified rules are identified, consistent, and associated with the specific CUI category._
3.1.9[b]	_Privacy and security notices are displayed._
3.1.10	**_Use session lock with pattern-hiding displays to prevent access/viewing of data after period of inactivity_**
3.1.10[a]	_The period of inactivity after which the system initiates a session lock is defined._
3.1.10[b]	_Access to the system and viewing of data is prevented by initiating a session lock after the defined period of inactivity._
3.1.10[c]	_Previously visible information is concealed via a pattern-hiding display after the defined period of inactivity._
3.1.11	**_Terminate (automatically) a user session after a defined condition_**
3.1.11[a]	_Conditions requiring a user session to terminate are defined._
3.1.11[b]	_A user session is automatically terminated after any of the defined conditions occur._

Control #	Description	Assessment Method*	Document (e.g., SSP or Co. Procedure Guide)	Page #	Reviewed By	Validated By
Access Control (AC)						
3.1.12	*Monitor and control remote access sessions*					
3.1.12[a]	*Remote access sessions are permitted.*					
3.1.12[b]	*The types of permitted remote access are identified.*					
3.1.12[c]	*Remote access sessions are controlled.*					
3.1.12[d]	*Remote access sessions are monitored.*					
3.1.13	*Employ cryptographic mechanisms to protect the confidentiality of remote access sessions*					
3.1.13[a]	*Cryptographic mechanisms to protect the confidentiality of remote access sessions are identified.*					
3.1.13[b]	*Cryptographic mechanisms to protect the confidentiality of remote access sessions are implemented.*					
3.1.14	*Route remote access via managed access control points*					
3.1.14[a]	*Managed access control points are identified and implemented.*					
3.1.14[b]	*Remote access is routed through managed network access control points.*					
3.1.15	*Authorize remote execution of privileged commands and remote access to security-relevant information*					
3.1.15[a]	*Privileged commands authorized for remote execution are identified.*					
3.1.15[b]	*Security-relevant information authorized to be accessed remotely is identified.*					
3.1.15[c]	*The execution of the identified privileged commands via remote access is authorized.*					
3.1.15[d]	*Access to the identified security-relevant information via remote access is authorized.*					
3.1.16	*Authorize wireless access prior to allowing such connections*					
3.1.16[a]	*Wireless access points are identified.*					
3.1.16[b]	*Wireless access is authorized prior to allowing such connections.*					

3.1.17	**Protect wireless access using authentication and encryption**
3.1.17[a]	Wireless access to the system is protected using authentication.
3.1.17[b]	Wireless access to the system is protected using encryption.
3.1.18	**Control connection of mobile devices**
3.1.18[a]	Mobile devices that process, store, or transmit CUI are identified.
3.1.18[b]	Mobile device connections are authorized.
3.1.18[c]	Mobile device connections are monitored and logged.
3.1.19	**Encrypt CUI on mobile devices**
3.1.19[a]	Mobile devices and mobile computing platforms that process, store, or transmit CUI are identified.
3.1.19[b]	Encryption is employed to protect CUI on identified mobile devices and mobile computing platforms.
3.1.20[a]	Connections to external systems are identified.
3.1.20[b]	The use of external systems is identified.
3.1.20[c]	Connections to external systems are verified.
3.1.20[d]	The use of external systems is verified.
3.1.20[e]	Connections to external systems are controlled/limited.
3.1.20[f]	The use of external systems is controlled/limited.
3.1.20[a]	Connections to external systems are identified.
3.1.21	**Limit use of organizational portable storage devices on external systems**
3.1.21[a]	The use of portable storage devices containing CUI on external systems is identified and documented.
3.1.21[b]	Limits on the use of portable storage devices containing CUI on external systems are defined.
3.1.21[c]	The use of portable storage devices containing CUI on external systems is limited as defined.

3.1.22	*Control CUI posted or processed on publicly accessible systems*	
3.1.22[a]	Individuals authorized to post or process information on publicly accessible systems are identified.	
3.1.22[b]	Procedures to ensure CUI is not posted or processed on publicly accessible systems are identified.	
3.1.22[c]	A review process is in place prior to posting of any content to publicly accessible systems.	
3.1.22[d]	Content on publicly accessible systems is reviewed to ensure that it does not include CUI.	
3.1.22[e]	Mechanisms are in place to remove and address improper posting of CUI.	
3.1.22[a]	Individuals authorized to post or process information on publicly accessible systems are identified.	

Control #	Description	Assessment Method*	Document (e.g., SSP or Co. Procedure Guide)	Page #	Reviewed By	Validated By
Awareness & Training (AT)						
3.2.1	*Ensure that managers, systems administrators, and users of organizational information systems are made aware of the security risks associated with their activities and of the applicable policies, standards, and procedures related to the security of organizational information systems*					
3.2.1[a]	*Security risks associated with organizational activities involving CUI are identified.*					
3.2.1[b]	*Policies, standards, and procedures related to the security of the system are identified.*					
3.2.1[c]	*Managers, systems administrators, and users of the system are made aware of the security risks associated with their activities.*					
3.2.1[d]	*Managers, systems administrators, and users of the system are made aware of the applicable policies, standards, and procedures related to the security of the system.*					
3.2.2	*Ensure that organizational personnel are adequately trained to carry out their assigned information security-related duties and responsibilities*					
3.2.2[a]	*Information security-related duties, roles, and responsibilities are defined.*					
3.2.2[b]	*Information security-related duties, roles, and responsibilities are assigned to designated personnel.*					
3.2.2[c]	*Personnel are adequately trained to carry out their assigned information security-related duties, roles, and responsibilities.*					
3.2.3	*Provide security awareness training on recognizing and reporting potential indicators of insider threat*					
3.2.3[a]	*Potential indicators associated with insider threats are identified.*					

3.2.3[b]	*Security awareness training on recognizing and reporting potential indicators of insider threat is provided to managers and employees.*	

Control #	Description	Assessment Method*	Document (e.g., SSP or Co: Procedure Guide)	Page #	Reviewed By	Validated By

Audit & Accountability (AU)

Control #	Description					
3.3.1	*Create, protect, and retain information system audit records to the extent needed to enable the monitoring, analysis, investigation, and reporting of unlawful, unauthorized, or inappropriate information system activity*					
3.3.1[a]	*Audit logs needed (i.e., event types to be logged) to enable the monitoring, analysis, investigation, and reporting of unlawful or unauthorized system activity are specified.*					
3.3.1[b]	*The content of audit records needed to support monitoring, analysis, investigation, and reporting of unlawful or unauthorized system activity is defined.*					
3.3.1[c]	*Audit records are created (generated).*					
3.3.1[d]	*Audit records, once created, contain the defined content.*					
3.3.1[e]	*Retention requirements for audit records are defined.*					
3.3.1[f]	*Audit records are retained as defined.*					
3.3.2	*Ensure that the actions of individual information system users can be uniquely traced to those users, so they can be held accountable for their actions*					
3.3.2[a]	*The content of the audit records needed to support the ability to uniquely trace users to their actions is defined.*					
3.3.2[b]	*Audit records, once created, contain the defined content.*					
3.3.3	*Review and update audited events*					
3.3.3[a]	*A process for determining when to review logged events is defined.*					
3.3.3[b]	*Event types being logged are reviewed in accordance with the defined review process.*					

3.3.3[c]	*Event types being logged are updated based on the review.*
3.3.4	**Alert in the event of an audit process failure**
3.3.4[a]	*Personnel or roles to be alerted in the event of an audit logging process failure are identified.*
3.3.4[b]	*Types of audit logging process failures for which alert will be generated are defined.*
3.3.4[c]	*Identified personnel or roles are alerted in the event of an audit logging process failure.*
3.3.5	**Correlate audit review, analysis, and reporting processes for investigation and response to indications of inappropriate, suspicious, or unusual activity**
3.3.5[a]	*Audit record review, analysis, and reporting processes for investigation and response to indications of unlawful, unauthorized, suspicious, or unusual activity are defined.*
3.3.5[b]	*Defined audit record review, analysis, and reporting processes are correlated.*
3.3.6	**Provide audit reduction and report generation to support on-demand analysis and reporting**
3.3.6[a]	*An audit record reduction capability that supports on-demand analysis is provided.*
3.3.6[b]	*A report generation capability that supports on-demand reporting is provided.*
3.3.7	**Provide an information system capability that compares and synchronizes internal system clocks with an authoritative source to generate time stamps for audit records**
3.3.7[a]	*Internal system clocks are used to generate time stamps for audit records.*
3.3.7[b]	*An authoritative source with which to compare and synchronize internal system clocks is specified.*
3.3.7[c]	*Internal system clocks used to generate time stamps for audit records are*

	compared to and synchronized with the specified authoritative time source.	
3.3.8	***Protect audit information and audit tools from unauthorized access, modification, and deletion***	
3.3.8[a]	*Audit information is protected from unauthorized access.*	
3.3.8[b]	*Audit information is protected from unauthorized modification.*	
3.3.8[c]	*Audit information is protected from unauthorized deletion.*	
3.3.8[d]	*Audit logging tools are protected from unauthorized access.*	
3.3.8[e]	*Audit logging tools are protected from unauthorized modification.*	
3.3.8[f]	*Audit logging tools are protected from unauthorized deletion.*	
3.3.9	***Limit management of audit functionality to a subset of privileged users***	
3.3.9[a]	*A subset of privileged users granted access to manage audit logging functionality is defined.*	
3.3.9[b]	*Management of audit logging functionality is limited to the defined subset of privileged users.*	

Control #	Description	Assessment Method*	Document (e.g., SSP or Co. Procedure Guide)	Page #	Reviewed By	Validated By
Configuration Management (CM)						
3.4.1	*Establish and maintain baseline configurations and inventories of organizational information systems (including hardware, software, firmware, and documentation) throughout the respective system development life cycles*					
3.4.1[a]	*A baseline configuration is established.*					
3.4.1[b]	*The baseline configuration includes hardware, software, firmware, and documentation.*					
3.4.1[c]	*The baseline configuration is maintained (reviewed and updated) throughout the system development life cycle.*					
3.4.1[d]	*A system inventory is established.*					
3.4.1[e]	*The system inventory includes hardware, software, firmware, and documentation.*					
3.4.1[f]	*The inventory is maintained (reviewed and updated) throughout the system development life cycle.*					
3.4.2	*Establish and enforce security configuration settings for information technology products employed in organizational information systems*					
3.4.2[a]	*Security configuration settings for information technology products employed in the system are established and included in the baseline configuration.*					
3.4.2[b]	*Security configuration settings for information technology products employed in the system are enforced.*					
3.4.3	*Track, review, approve/disapprove, and audit changes to information systems*					
3.4.3[a]	*Changes to the system are tracked.*					
3.4.3[b]	*Changes to the system are reviewed.*					

3.4.3[c]	*Changes to the system are approved or disapproved.*	
3.4.3[d]	*Changes to the system are logged.*	
3.4.4	**Analyze the security impact of changes prior to implementation**	
3.4.5	**Define, document, approve, and enforce physical and logical access restrictions associated with changes to the information system**	
3.4.5[a]	*Physical access restrictions associated with changes to the system are defined.*	
3.4.5[b]	*Physical access restrictions associated with changes to the system are documented.*	
3.4.5[c]	*Physical access restrictions associated with changes to the system are approved.*	
3.4.5[d]	*Physical access restrictions associated with changes to the system are enforced.*	
3.4.5[e]	*Logical access restrictions associated with changes to the system are defined.*	
3.4.5[f]	*Logical access restrictions associated with changes to the system are documented.*	
3.4.5[g]	*Logical access restrictions associated with changes to the system are approved.*	
3.4.5[h]	*Logical access restrictions associated with changes to the system are enforced.*	
3.4.6	**Employ the principle of least functionality by configuring the information system to provide only essential capabilities**	
3.4.6[a]	*Essential system capabilities are defined based on the principle of least functionality.*	
3.4.6[b]	*The system is configured to provide only the defined essential capabilities.*	
3.4.7	**Restrict, disable, and prevent the use of nonessential programs, functions, ports, protocols, and services**	

3.4.7[a]	*Essential programs are defined.*
3.4.7[b]	*The use of nonessential programs is defined.*
3.4.7[c]	*The use of nonessential programs is restricted, disabled, or prevented as defined.*
3.4.7[d]	*Essential functions are defined.*
3.4.7[e]	*The use of nonessential functions is defined.*
3.4.7[f]	*The use of nonessential functions is restricted, disabled, or prevented as defined.*
3.4.7[g]	*Essential ports are defined.*
3.4.7[h]	*The use of nonessential ports is defined.*
3.4.7[i]	*The use of nonessential ports is restricted, disabled, or prevented as defined.*
3.4.7[j]	*Essential protocols are defined.*
3.4.7[k]	*The use of nonessential protocols is defined.*
3.4.7[l]	*The use of nonessential protocols is restricted, disabled, or prevented as defined.*
3.4.7[m]	*Essential services are defined.*
3.4.7[n]	*The use of nonessential services is defined.*
3.4.7[o]	*The use of nonessential services is restricted, disabled, or prevented as defined.*
3.4.8	**Apply deny-by-exception (blacklist) policy to prevent the use of unauthorized software or deny all, permit-by-exception (whitelisting) policy to allow the execution of authorized software**
3.4.8[a]	*A policy specifying whether whitelisting or blacklisting is to be implemented is specified.*
3.4.8[b]	*The software allowed to execute under whitelisting or denied use under blacklisting is specified.*
3.4.8[c]	*Whitelisting to allow the execution of authorized software or blacklisting to prevent the use of unauthorized software is implemented as specified.*
3.4.9	**Control and monitor user-installed software**
3.4.9[a]	*A policy for controlling the installation of software by users is established.*

3.4.9[b]	Installation of software by users is controlled based on the established policy.	
3.4.9[c]	Installation of software by users is monitored.	

Control #	Description	Assessment Method*	Document (e.g., SSP or Co. Procedure Guide)	Page #	Reviewed By	Validated By
Identification & Authentication (IA)						
3.5.1	*Identify information system users, processes acting on behalf of users, or devices*					
3.5.1[a]	*System users are identified.*					
3.5.1[b]	*Processes acting on behalf of users are identified.*					
3.5.1[c]	*Devices accessing the system are identified.*					
3.5.2	*Authenticate (or verify) the identities of those users, processes, or devices, as a prerequisite to allowing access to organizational information systems*					
3.5.2[a]	*The identity of each user is authenticated or verified as a prerequisite to system access.*					
3.5.2[b]	*The identity of each process acting on behalf of a user is authenticated or verified as a prerequisite to system access.*					
3.5.2[c]	*The identity of each device accessing or connecting to the system is authenticated or verified as a prerequisite to system access.*					
3.5.3	*Use multifactor authentication for local and network access to privileged accounts and for network access to non-privileged accounts*					
3.5.3[a]	*Privileged accounts are identified.*					
3.5.3[b]	*Multifactor authentication is implemented for local access to privileged accounts.*					
3.5.3[c]	*Multifactor authentication is implemented for network access to privileged accounts.*					
3.5.3[d]	*Multifactor authentication is implemented for network access to non-privileged accounts.*					

3.5.4	*Employ replay-resistant authentication mechanisms for network access to privileged and nonprivileged accounts*	
3.5.5	***Prevent reuse of identifiers for a defined period***	
3.5.5[a]	*A period within which identifiers cannot be reused is defined.*	
3.5.5[b]	*Reuse of identifiers is prevented within the defined period.*	
3.5.6	***Disable identifiers after a defined period of inactivity***	
3.5.6[a]	*A period of inactivity after which an identifier is disabled is defined.*	
3.5.6[b]	*Identifiers are disabled after the defined period of inactivity.*	
3.5.7	***Enforce a minimum password complexity and change of characters when new passwords are created***	
3.5.7[a]	*Password complexity requirements are defined.*	
3.5.7[b]	*Password change of character requirements are defined.*	
3.5.7[c]	*Minimum password complexity requirements as defined are enforced when new passwords are created.*	
3.5.7[d]	*Minimum password change of character requirements as defined are enforced when new passwords are created.*	
3.5.8	***Prohibit password reuse for a specified number of generations***	
3.5.8[a]	*The number of generations during which a password cannot be reused is specified.*	
3.5.8[b]	*Reuse of passwords is prohibited during the specified number of generations.*	
3.5.9	***Allow temporary password use for system logons with an immediate change to a permanent password***	

3.5.10	Store and transmit only encrypted representation of passwords	
3.5.10[a]	Passwords are cryptographically protected in storage.	
3.5.10[b]	Passwords are cryptographically protected in transit.	
3.5.11.	Obscure feedback of authentication information	

Control #	Description	Assessment Method*	Document (e.g., SSP or Co. Procedure Guide)	Page #	Reviewed By	Validated By
Incident Response (IR)						
3.6.1	**Establish an operational incident-handling capability for organizational information systems that includes adequate preparation, detection, analysis, containment, recovery, and user response activities**					
3.6.1[a]	An operational incident-handling capability is established.					
3.6.1[b]	The operational incident-handling capability includes preparation.					
3.6.1[c]	The operational incident-handling capability includes detection.					
3.6.1[d]	The operational incident-handling capability includes analysis.					
3.6.1[e]	The operational incident-handling capability includes containment.					
3.6.1[f]	The operational incident-handling capability includes recovery.					
3.6.1[g]	The operational incident-handling capability includes user response activities.					
3.6.2	**Track, document, and report incidents to appropriate officials and/or authorities both internal and external to the organization**					
3.6.2[a]	Incidents are tracked.					
3.6.2[b]	Incidents are documented.					
3.6.2[c]	Authorities to whom incidents are to be reported are identified.					
3.6.2[d]	Organizational officials to whom incidents are to be reported are identified.					
3.6.2[e]	Identified authorities are notified of incidents.					
3.6.2[f]	Identified organizational officials are notified of incidents.					
3.6.3	**Test the organizational incident response capability**					

Control #	Description	Assessment Method*	Document (e.g., SSP or Co. Procedure Guide)	Page #	Reviewed By	Valid ated By
Maintenance (MA)						
3.7.1	*Perform maintenance on organizational information systems*					
3.7.2	*Provide effective controls on the tools, techniques, mechanisms, and personnel used to conduct information system maintenance*					
3.7.2[a]	Tools used to conduct system maintenance are controlled.					
3.7.2[b]	Techniques used to conduct system maintenance are controlled.					
3.7.2[c]	Mechanisms used to conduct system maintenance are controlled.					
3.7.2[d]	Personnel used to conduct system maintenance are controlled.					
3.7.3	Ensure equipment removed for off-site maintenance is sanitized of any CUI					
3.7.4	*Check media containing diagnostic and test programs for malicious code before the media are used in the information system*					
3.7.5	*Require multifactor authentication to establish nonlocal maintenance sessions via external network connections and terminate such connections when nonlocal maintenance is complete*					
3.7.5[a]	Multifactor authentication is used to establish nonlocal maintenance sessions via external network connections.					
3.7.5[b]	Nonlocal maintenance sessions established via external network connections are terminated when nonlocal maintenance is complete.					

| 3.7.6 | *Supervise the maintenance activities of maintenance personnel without required access authorization* |

Control #	Description	Assessment Method*	Document (e.g., SSP or Co. Procedure Guide)	Page #	Reviewed By	Validated By
Media Protection (MP)						
3.8.1	*Protect (i.e., physically control and securely store) information system media containing CUI, both paper and digital*					
3.8.1[a]	*Paper media containing CUI is physically controlled.*					
3.8.1[b]	*Digital media containing CUI is physically controlled.*					
3.8.1[c]	*Paper media containing CUI is securely stored.*					
3.8.1[d]	*Digital media containing CUI is securely stored.*					
3.8.2	*Limit access to CUI on information system media to authorized users*					
3.8.3	*Sanitize or destroy information system media containing CUI before disposal or release for reuse*					
3.8.3[a]	*System media containing CUI is sanitized or destroyed before disposal.*					
3.8.3[b]	*System media containing CUI is sanitized before it is released for reuse.*					
3.8.4	*Mark media with necessary CUI markings and distribution limitations*					
3.8.4[a]	*Media containing CUI is marked with applicable CUI markings.*					
3.8.4[b]	*Media containing CUI is marked with distribution limitations.*					
3.8.5	*Control access to media containing CUI and maintain accountability for media during transport outside of controlled areas*					
3.8.5[a]	*Access to media containing CUI is controlled.*					
3.8.5[b]	*Accountability for media containing CUI is maintained during transport outside of controlled areas.*					

3.8.6	*Implement cryptographic mechanisms to protect the confidentiality of CUI stored on digital media during transport unless otherwise protected by alternative physical safeguards*
3.8.7	*Control the use of removable media on information system components*
3.8.8	*Prohibit the use of portable storage devices when such devices have no identifiable owner*
3.8.9	*Protect the confidentiality of backup CUI at storage locations*

Control #	Description	Assessment Method*	Document (e.g., SSP or Co. Procedure Guide)	Page #	Reviewed By	Validated By
Personnel Security (PS)						
3.9.1	*Screen individuals prior to authorizing access to information systems containing CUI*					
3.9.2	*Ensure that CUI and information systems containing CUI are protected during and after personnel actions such as terminations and transfers*					
3.9.2[a]	*A policy and/or process for terminating system access and any credentials coincident with personnel actions is established.*					
3.9.2[b]	*System access and credentials are terminated consistent with personnel actions such as termination or transfer.*					
3.9.2[c]	*The system is protected during and after personnel transfer actions.*					

Control #	Description	Assessment Method*	Document (e.g., SSP or Co. Procedure Guide)	Page #	Reviewed By	Validated By
Physical Security (PP)						
3.10.1	**Limit physical access to organizational information systems, equipment, and the respective operating environments to authorized individuals**					
3.10.1[a]	Authorized individuals allowed physical access are identified.					
3.10.1[b]	Physical access to organizational systems is limited to authorized individuals.					
3.10.1[c]	Physical access to equipment is limited to authorized individuals.					
3.10.1[d]	Physical access to operating environments is limited to authorized individuals.					
3.10.2	**Protect and monitor the physical facility and support infrastructure for those information systems**					
3.10.2[a]	The physical facility where organizational systems reside is protected.					
3.10.2[b]	The support infrastructure for organizational systems is protected.					
3.10.2[c]	The physical facility where organizational systems reside is monitored.					
3.10.2[d]	The support infrastructure for organizational systems is monitored.					
3.10.3	**Escort visitors and monitor visitor activity**					
3.10.3[a]	Visitors are escorted.					
3.10.3[b]	Visitor activity is monitored.					
3.10.4	**Maintain audit logs of physical access**					
3.10.5	**Control and manage physical access devices**					
3.10.5[a]	Physical access devices are identified.					
3.10.5[b]	Physical access devices are controlled.					
3.10.5[c]	Physical access devices are managed.					

3.10.6	Enforce safeguarding measures for CUI at alternate work sites (e.g., telework sites)	
3.10.6[a]	Safeguarding measures for CUI are defined for alternate work sites.	
3.10.6[b]	Safeguarding measures for CUI are enforced for alternate work sites.	

Control #	Description	Assessment Method*	Document (e.g., SSP or Co. Procedure Guide)	Page #	Reviewed By	Validated By
Risk Assessments (RA)						
3.11.1	**Periodically assess the risk to organizational operations (including mission, functions, image, or reputation), organizational assets, and individuals, resulting from the operation of organizational information systems and the associated processing, storage, or transmission of CUI**					
3.11.1[a]	The frequency to assess risk to organizational operations, organizational assets, and individuals is defined.					
3.11.1[b]	Risk to organizational operations, organizational assets, and individuals resulting from the operation of an organizational system that processes, stores, or transmits CUI is assessed with the defined frequency.					
3.11.2	**Scan for vulnerabilities in the information system and applications periodically and when new vulnerabilities affecting the system are identified**					
3.11.2[a]	The frequency to scan for vulnerabilities in organizational systems and applications is defined.					
3.11.2[b]	Vulnerability scans are performed on organizational systems with the defined frequency.					
3.11.2[c]	Vulnerability scans are performed on applications with the defined frequency.					
3.11.2[d]	Vulnerability scans are performed on organizational systems when new vulnerabilities are identified.					
3.11.2[e]	Vulnerability scans are performed on applications when new vulnerabilities are identified.					

3.11.3	Remediate vulnerabilities in accordance with assessments of risk	
3.11.3[a]	Vulnerabilities are identified.	
3.11.3[b]	Vulnerabilities are remediated in accordance with risk assessments.	

Control #	Description	Assessment Method*	Document (e.g., SSP or Co. Procedure Guide)	Page #	Reviewed By	Validated By
Security Assessments (SA)						
3.12.1	**Periodically assess the security controls in organizational information systems to determine if the controls are effective in their application**					
3.12.1[a]	The frequency of security control assessments is defined.					
3.12.1[b]	Security controls are assessed with the defined frequency to determine if the controls are effective in their application.					
3.12.2	*Develop and implement plans of action designed to correct deficiencies and reduce or eliminate vulnerabilities in organizational information systems*					
3.12.2[a]	Deficiencies and vulnerabilities to be addressed by the plan of action are identified.					
3.12.2[b]	A plan of action is developed to correct identified deficiencies and reduce or eliminate identified vulnerabilities.					
3.12.2[c]	The plan of action is implemented to correct identified deficiencies and reduce or eliminate identified vulnerabilities.					
3.12.3	*Monitor information system security controls on an ongoing basis to ensure the continued effectiveness of the controls*					
3.12.4	*Develop, document, and periodically update system security plans that describe system boundaries, system environments of operation, how security requirements are implemented, and the relationships with or connections to other systems*					

3.12.4[a]	A system security plan is developed.	
3.12.4[b]	The system boundary is described and documented in the system security plan.	
3.12.4[c]	The system environment of operation is described and documented in the system security plan.	
3.12.4[d]	The security requirements identified and approved by the designated authority as non-applicable are identified.	
3.12.4[e]	The method of security requirement implementation is described and documented in the system security plan.	
3.12.4[f]	The relationship with or connection to other systems is described and documented in the system security plan.	
3.12.4[g]	The frequency to update the system security plan is defined.	
3.12.4[h]	System security plan is updated with the defined frequency.	

Control #	Description	Assessment Method*	Document (e.g., SSP or Co. Procedure Guide)	Page #	Reviewed By	Validated By
System & Communications Protection (SC)						
3.13.1	***Monitor, control, and protect organizational communications (i.e., information transmitted or received by organizational information systems) at the external boundaries and key internal boundaries of the information systems***					
3.13.1[a]	*The external system boundary is defined.*					
3.13.1[b]	*Key internal system boundaries are defined.*					
3.13.1[c]	*Communications are monitored at the external system boundary.*					
3.13.1[d]	*Communications are monitored at key internal boundaries.*					
3.13.1[e]	*Communications are controlled at the external system boundary.*					
3.13.1[f]	*Communications are controlled at key internal boundaries.*					
3.13.1[g]	*Communications are protected at the external system boundary.*					
3.13.1[h]	*Communications are protected at key internal boundaries.*					
3.13.2	***Employ architectural designs, software development techniques, and systems engineering principles that promote effective information security within organizational information systems***					
3.13.2[a]	*Architectural designs that promote effective information security are identified.*					
3.13.2[b]	*Software development techniques that promote effective information security are identified.*					
3.13.2[c]	*Systems engineering principles that promote effective information security are identified.*					

3.13.2[d]	*Identified architectural designs that promote effective information security are employed.*
3.13.2[e]	*Identified software development techniques that promote effective information security are employed.*
3.13.2[f]	*Identified systems engineering principles that promote effective information security are employed.*
3.13.3	**Separate user functionality from information system management functionality**
3.13.3[a]	*User functionality is identified.*
3.13.3[b]	*System management functionality is identified.*
3.13.3[c]	*User functionality is separated from system management functionality.*
3.13.4	**Prevent unauthorized and unintended information transfer via shared system resources**
3.13.5	**Implement subnetworks for publicly accessible system components that are physically or logically separated from internal networks**
3.13.5[a]	*Publicly accessible system components are identified.*
3.13.5[b]	*Subnetworks for publicly accessible system components are physically or logically separated from internal networks.*
3.13.6	**Deny network communications traffic by default and allow network communications traffic by exception (i.e., deny all, permit by exception)**
3.13.6[a]	*Network communications traffic is denied by default.*
3.13.6[b]	*Network communications traffic is allowed by exception.*
3.13.7	**Prevent remote devices from simultaneously establishing non-remote connections with the information system and communicating via some other connection to resources in external networks**

Control #	Description	Assessment Method*	Document (e.g., SSP or Co. Procedure Guide)	Page #	Reviewed By	Validated By
System & Communications Protection (SC)						
3.13.8	**Implement cryptographic mechanisms to prevent unauthorized disclosure of CUI during transmission unless otherwise protected by alternative physical safeguards**					
3.13.8[a]	Cryptographic mechanisms intended to prevent unauthorized disclosure of CUI are identified.					
3.13.8[b]	Alternative physical safeguards intended to prevent unauthorized disclosure of CUI are identified.					
3.13.8[c]	Either cryptographic mechanisms or alternative physical safeguards are implemented to prevent unauthorized disclosure of CUI during transmission.					
3.13.9	**Terminate network connections associated with communications sessions at the end of the sessions or after a defined period of inactivity**					
3.13.9[a]	A period of inactivity to terminate network connections associated with communications sessions is defined.					
3.13.9[b]	Network connections associated with communications sessions are terminated at the end of the sessions.					
3.13.9[c]	Network connections associated with communications sessions are terminated after the defined period of inactivity.					
3.13.10	**Establish and manage cryptographic keys for cryptography employed in the information system**					
3.13.10[a]	Cryptographic keys are established whenever cryptography is employed.					
3.13.10[b]	Cryptographic keys are managed whenever cryptography is employed.					
3.13.11	**Employ FIPS-validated cryptography when used to protect the confidentiality of CUI**					

3.13.12	**Prohibit remote activation of collaborative computing devices and provide indication of devices in use to users present at the device**
3.13.12[a]	Collaborative computing devices are identified.
3.13.12[b]	Collaborative computing devices provide indication to users of devices in use.
3.13.12[c]	Remote activation of collaborative computing devices is prohibited.
3.13.13	**Control and monitor the use of mobile code**
3.13.13[a]	Use of mobile code is controlled.
3.13.13[b]	Use of mobile code is monitored.
3.13.14	**Control and monitor the use of Voice over Internet Protocol (VoIP) technologies**
3.13.14[a]	Use of Voice over Internet Protocol (VoIP) technologies is controlled.
3.13.14[b]	Use of Voice over Internet Protocol (VoIP) technologies is monitored.
3.13.15	**Protect the authenticity of communications sessions**
3.13.16	**Protect the confidentiality of CUI at rest**

Control #	Description	Assessment Method*	Document	Page #	Reviewed By	Validated By
System & Information Integrity (SI)						
3.14.1	*Identify, report, and correct information and information system flaws in a timely manner*					
3.14.1[a]	*The time within which to identify system flaws is specified.*					
3.14.1[b]	*System flaws are identified within the specified time frame.*					
3.14.1[c]	*The time within which to report system flaws is specified.*					
3.14.1[d]	*System flaws are reported within the specified time frame.*					
3.14.1[e]	*The time within which to correct system flaws is specified.*					
3.14.1[f]	*System flaws are corrected within the specified time frame.*					
3.14.2	*Provide protection from malicious code at appropriate locations within organizational information systems*					
3.14.2[a]	*Designated locations for malicious code protection are identified.*					
3.14.2[b]	*Protection from malicious code at designated locations is provided.*					
3.14.3	*Monitor information system security alerts and advisories and take appropriate actions in response*					
3.14.3[a]	*Response actions to system security alerts and advisories are identified.*					
3.14.3[b]	*System security alerts and advisories are monitored.*					
3.14.3[c]	*Actions in response to system security alerts and advisories are taken.*					
3.14.4	*Update malicious code protection mechanisms when new releases are available*					
3.14.5	*Perform periodic scans of the information system and real-time scans of files from external sources as files are*					

	downloaded, opened, or executed	
3.14.5[a]	*The frequency for malicious code scans is defined.*	
3.14.5[b]	*Malicious code scans are performed with the defined frequency.*	
3.14.5[c]	*Real-time malicious code scans of files from external sources as files are downloaded, opened, or executed are performed.*	
3.14.6	**Monitor the information system including inbound and outbound communications traffic, to detect attacks and indicators of potential attacks**	
3.14.6[a]	*The system is monitored to detect attacks and indicators of potential attacks.*	
3.14.6[b]	*Inbound communications traffic is monitored to detect attacks and indicators of potential attacks.*	
3.14.6[c]	*Outbound communications traffic is monitored to detect attacks and indicators of potential attacks.*	
3.14.7	**Identify unauthorized use of the information system**	
3.14.7[a]	*Authorized use of the system is defined.*	
3.14.7[b]	*Unauthorized use of the system is identified.*	

About the Author

Mr. Russo is currently the Senior Information Security Engineer within the Department of Defense's (DOD) F-35 Joint Strike Fighter program. He has an extensive background in cybersecurity and is an expert in the Risk Management Framework (RMF) and DOD Instruction 8510 which implements RMF throughout the DOD and the federal government. He holds both a Certified Information Systems Security Professional (CISSP) certification and a CISSP in information security architecture (ISSAP). He holds a 2017 certification as a Chief Information Security Officer (CISO) from the National Defense University, Washington, DC. He retired from the US Army Reserves in 2012 as the Senior Intelligence Officer.

He is the former CISO at the Department of Education wherein 2016 he led the effort to close over 95% of the outstanding US Congressional and Inspector General cybersecurity shortfall weaknesses spanning as far back as five years.

Mr. Russo is the former Senior Cybersecurity Engineer supporting the Joint Medical Logistics Development Functional Center of the Defense Health Agency (DHA) at Fort Detrick, MD. He led a team of engineering and cybersecurity professionals protecting five major Medical Logistics systems supporting over 200 DOD Medical Treatment Facilities around the globe.

In 2011, Mr. Russo was certified by the Office of Personnel Management as a graduate of the Senior Executive Service Candidate program.

From 2009 through 2011, Mr. Russo was the Chief Technology Officer at the Small Business Administration (SBA). He led a team of over 100 IT professionals in supporting an intercontinental Enterprise IT infrastructure and security operations spanning 12-time zones; he deployed cutting-edge technologies to enhance SBA's business and information sharing operations supporting the small business community. Mr. Russo was the first-ever Program Executive Officer (PEO)/Senior Program Manager in the Office of Intelligence & Analysis at Headquarters, Department of Homeland Security (DHS), Washington, DC. Mr. Russo was responsible for the development and deployment of secure Information and Intelligence support systems for OI&A to include software applications and systems to enhance the DHS mission. He was responsible for the program management development lifecycle during his tenure at DHS.

He holds a Master of Science from the National Defense University in Government Information Leadership with a concentration in Cybersecurity and a Bachelor of Arts in Political Science with a minor in Russian Studies from Lehigh University. He holds Level III Defense Acquisition certification in Program Management, Information Technology, and Systems Engineering. He has been a member of the DOD Acquisition Corps since 2001.

The following supplements now available on Amazon

System Security Plan (SSP) Template & Workbook NIST-based

https://www.amazon.com/System-Security-Plan-Template-Workbook-ebook/dp/B07BCY41D2/ref=sr_1_1?ie=UTF8&qid=1523490730&sr=8-1&keywords=system+security+plan

NIST 800-171: Writing an Effective Plan of Action & Milestones (POAM)

https://www.amazon.com/NIST-800-171-Milestones-Understanding-Responsibilities-ebook/dp/B07C9T3ZCT/ref=sr_1_1?ie=UTF8&qid=1523491061&sr=8-1&keywords=plan+of+action+and+milestone

www.ingramcontent.com/pod-product-compliance
Lightning Source LLC
Chambersburg PA
CBHW032211220526
45472CB00018B/874